THE PHILOSOPHY OF FREEDOM

The Philosophy of Freedom

(The Philosophy of Spiritual Activity)

THE BASIS FOR A MODERN WORLD CONCEPTION

Some results of introspective observation following the methods of Natural Science

RUDOLF STEINER

Seventh English edition:
Translated from the German, and with an Introduction
by Michael Wilson

RUDOLF STEINER PRESS

Rudolf Steiner Press
Hillside House, The Square
Forest Row, East Sussex
RH18 5ES

www.rudolfsteinerpress.com

Seventh English edition 1964
Reprinted 1999, 2001, 2006

Originally published in German in 1894 under the title *Die Philosophie der Freiheit* (volume 4 in the *Rudolf Steiner Gesamtausgabe* or Collected Works) by Rudolf Steiner Verlag, Dornach. This authorized translation is published by kind permission of the Rudolf Steiner Nachlassverwaltung, Dornach

A catalogue record for this book is available from the British Library

ISBN-10: 1 85584 082 0
ISBN-13: 978 185584 082 9

Cover design by Andrew Morgan
Printed and bound in Great Britain by Cromwell Press Limited, Trowbridge, Wiltshire

CONTENTS

v

INTRODUCTION

RUDOLF STEINER was born in 1861 and died in 1925. In his autobiography, *The Course of My Life*,[1] he makes quite clear that the problems dealt with in *The Philosophy of Freedom* played a leading part in his life.

His childhood was spent in the Austrian countryside, where his father was a stationmaster. At the age of eight Steiner was already aware of things and beings that are not seen as well as those that are. Writing about his experiences at this age, he said, ". . . the reality of the spiritual world was as certain to me as that of the physical. I felt the need, however, for a sort of justification for this assumption."

Recognizing the boy's ability, his father sent him to the *Realschule* at Wiener Neustadt, and later to the Technical University in Vienna. Here Steiner had to support himself, by means of scholarships and tutoring. Studying and mastering many more subjects than were in his curriculum, he always came back to the problem of knowledge itself. He was very much aware that in the experience of oneself as an ego, one is in the world of the spirit. Although he took part in all the social activities going on around him—in the arts, the sciences, even in politics—he wrote that "much more vital at that time was the need to find an answer to the question: How far is it possible to prove that in human thinking real spirit is the agent?"

He made a deep study of philosophy, particularly the writings of Kant, but nowhere did he find a way of thinking that could be carried as far as a perception of the spiritual world. Thus Steiner was led to develop a theory of knowledge out of his own striving after truth, one which took its start from a direct experience of the spiritual nature of thinking.

As a student, Steiner's scientific ability was acknowledged when he was asked to edit Goethe's writings on nature. In Goethe he recognized one who had been able to perceive the spiritual in nature, even though he had not carried this as far as a direct perception of the spirit. Steiner was able to bring a new understanding to Goethe's scientific work through this insight into his perception of nature. Since no existing philosophical theory could take this kind of vision into account, and since Goethe had never stated

[1] Published in parts from 1923-5, and never completed. The titles given for Dr Steiner's books are those of the English translations.

explicitly what his philosophy of life was, Steiner filled this need by publishing, in 1886, an introductory book called *The Theory of Knowledge Implicit in Goethe's World-Conception*. His introductions to the several volumes and sections of Goethe's scientific writings (1883-97) have been collected into the book *Goethe the Scientist*. These are valuable contributions to the philosophy of science.

During this time his thoughts about his own philosophy were gradually coming to maturity. In the year 1888 he met Eduard von Hartmann, with whom he had already had a long correspondence. He describes the chilling effect on him of the way this philosopher of pessimism denied that thinking could ever reach reality, but must forever deal with illusions. Steiner was already clear in his mind how such obstacles were to be overcome. He did not stop at the problem of knowledge, but carried his ideas from this realm into the field of ethics, to help him deal with the problem of human freedom. He wanted to show that morality could be given a sure foundation without basing it upon imposed rules of conduct.

Meanwhile his work of editing had taken him away from his beloved Vienna to Weimar. Here Steiner wrestled with the task of presenting his ideas to the world. His observations of the spiritual had all the exactness of a science, and yet his experience of the reality of ideas was in some ways akin to the mystic's experience. Mysticism presents the intensity of immediate knowledge with conviction, but deals only with subjective impressions; it fails to deal with the reality outside man. Science, on the other hand, consists of ideas about the world, even if the ideas are mainly materialistic. By starting from the spiritual nature of thinking, Steiner was able to form ideas that bear upon the spiritual world in the same way that the ideas of natural science bear upon the physical. Thus he could describe his philosophy as the result of "introspective observation following the methods of Natural Science." He first presented an outline of his ideas in his doctoral dissertation, *Truth and Knowledge*, which bore the sub-title "Prelude to a 'Philosophy of Freedom'."

In 1894 *The Philosophy of Freedom* was published, and the content which had formed the centre of his life's striving was placed before the world. Steiner was deeply disappointed at the lack of understanding it received. Hartmann's reaction was typical; instead of accepting the discovery that thinking can lead to the reality of the spirit in the world, he continued to think that "spirit" was merely a concept existing in the human mind, and freedom an illusion based on ignorance. Such was fundamentally the view of the age to which Steiner introduced his philosophy. But however it seemed to others, Steiner had in fact established a firm foundation for knowledge of the spirit, and now he felt able to pursue his researches in this field without restraint. The *Philosophy of Freedom* summed up the ideas he had formed to deal with the riddles of existence that had so far dominated his life. "The further way," he wrote, "could now be nothing else but a struggle to find the right form of ideas to express the spiritual world itself."

While still at Weimar, Steiner wrote two more books, *Friedrich Nietzsche, Fighter for Freedom* (1895), inspired by a visit to the aged philosopher, and *Goethe's Conception of the World* (1897), which completed his work in this field. He then moved to Berlin to take over the editing of a literary magazine; here he wrote *Riddles of Philosophy* (1901) and *Mysticism and Modern Thought* (1901). He also embarked on an ever-increasing activity of lecturing. But his real task lay in deepening his knowledge of the spiritual world until he could reach the point of publishing the results of this research.

The rest of his life was devoted to building up a complete science of the spirit, to which he gave the name Anthroposophy. Foremost amongst his discoveries was his direct experience of the reality of the Christ, which soon took a central place in his whole teaching. The many books and lectures which he published set forth the magnificent scope of his vision.[2] From 1911 he turned also to the arts—drama, painting, architecture, eurythmy—showing the creative forming powers that can be drawn from spiritual vision. As a response to the disaster of the 1914-18 war, he showed how the social sphere could be given new life through an insight into the nature of man, his initiative bearing practical fruit in the fields of education, agriculture, therapy and medicine. After a few more years of intense activity, now as the leader of a world-wide movement, he died, leaving behind him an achievement that must allow his recognition as the first Initiate of the age of science.[3] Anthroposophy is itself a science, firmly based on the results of

[2] The list of titles is long, but the more important books include *Christianity as Mystical Fact* (1902), *Knowledge of the Higher Worlds and its Attainment* (1904), *Theosophy*, a description of the nature of man and his relation to the spiritual world (1904), and *Occult Science—An Outline*, an account of the evolution of man and the universe in terms of spiritual realities (1910).

[3] For an account of the life and work of Rudolf Steiner, see *A Scientist of the Invisible*, by A. P. Shepherd (1954). The range of his contribution to modern thought can be seen in *The Faithful Thinker*, edited by A. C. Harwood (1961).

observation, and open to investigation by anyone who is prepared to follow the path of development he pioneered—a path that takes its start from the struggle for inner freedom set forth in this book.

*   *   *

THE PHILOSOPHY OF FREEDOM can be seen as the crowning achievement of nineteenth-century philosophy. It answers all the problems of knowledge and morality that philosophers had raised, argued over, and eventually left unsolved with the conclusion that "we can never know". Yet this great achievement received no recognition, and only when Steiner had acquired a large following of people thankful for all that he had given them of his spiritual revelation, did there arise the desire to read also his earlier work, upon which he always insisted his whole research was firmly based. Perhaps if Steiner had spent the rest of his life expounding his philosophy, he would today be recognized throughout the world as a major philosopher; yet his achievement in going forward himself to develop the science of the spirit is much the greater, and this will surely be recognized in time. Indeed, philosophy has got itself a bad name, perhaps from its too-frequent negative results, and it might even be better to consider the *Philosophy of Freedom* not just as a chapter of philosophy, but as the key to a whole way of life.

Considered just as a piece of philosophy, it might in any case be thought out of date, having only historical interest. For instance, a modern scientist may well believe that any philosopher who spoke up against atomism has been proved wrong by the success of atomic physics. But this would be to misunderstand the nature of philosophy. Steiner deals in turn with each possible point of view, illustrating each one with an example from the literature, and then showing the fallacies or shortcomings that have to be overcome. Atomism is justified only so long as it is taken as an aid to the intellect in dealing with the forces of nature; it is wrong if it postulates qualities of a kind that belong to perceived phenomena, but attributes them to a realm that by definition can never be perceived. This mistaken view of the atom may have been abandoned by science, but it still persists in many quarters. Similarly, many of the old philosophical points of view, dating back to Kant, survive among scientists who are very advanced in the experimental or theoretical fields, so that Steiner's treatment of the problem of knowledge is still relevant. Confusion concerning the nature of perception is widespread, because of the reluctance to consider the central part played by thinking. Thinking is all too often dismissed as "subjective" and hence unreliable, without any realization that it is thinking itself that has made this decision. The belief that science can deal only with the "objective" world has led to the position where many scientists are quite unable to say whether the real world is the familiar world of their surroundings, as experienced through the senses and pictured in the imagination, or the theoretical world of spinning particles, imperceptible forces and statistical probabilities that is inferred from their experimental results.[4] Here Steiner's path of knowledge can give a firmer basis for natural science than it has ever had before, as well as providing a sure foundation for the development of spiritual science. Although there are many people who find all that they need in contemplating the wonders of the spiritual world, the *Philosophy of Freedom* does not exist mainly to provide a philosophical justification for their belief; its main value lies in the sound basis it can give to those who cannot bring themselves to accept anything that is not clearly scientific—a basis for knowledge, for self-knowledge, for moral action, for life itself. It does not "tell us what to do", but it opens a way to the spirit for all those for whom the scientific path to truth, rather than the mystical, is the only possibility.

Today we hear about the "free world" and the "value of the individual", and yet the current scientific view of man seems to lend little support to these concepts, but seems rather to lead to a kind of morality in which every type of behaviour is excused on the plea that "I cannot help being what I am!" If we would really value the individual, and support our feeling of freedom with knowledge, we must find a point of view which will lead the ego to help itself become what it wants to be—a free being. This cannot mean that we must abandon the scientific path; only that the scope of science must be widened to take into account the ego that experiences itself as spirit, which it does in the act of thinking. Thus the *Philosophy of Freedom* takes its start by examining the process of thinking, and shows that there need be no fear of unknown causes in unknown worlds forever beyond the reach of our knowledge, since limits to knowledge exist only in so far as we fail to awaken our thinking to the point where it becomes an organ of direct perception. Having established the possibility of knowing, the book goes on to show that we can also know the causes of our actions, and if our motive for acting comes from pure intuition, from thinking alone, without any promptings from the appearances and

[4] See the discussion by Owen Barfield in "Saving the Appearances", (1957).

illusions of the sense-world, then we can indeed act in freedom, out of pure love for the deed.

Man ultimately has his fate in his own hands, though the path to this condition of freedom is a long and a hard one, in the course of which he must develop merciless knowledge of himself and selfless understanding of others. He must, through his own labours, give birth to what St Paul called "the second Adam that was made a quickening spirit". Indeed Steiner himself has referred to his philosophy of freedom as a Pauline theory of knowledge.

Notes on the translation

This book was first translated into English by Professor and Mrs R. F. Alfred Hoernlé, in 1916, and was edited by Mr Harry Collison, who wrote that he was fortunate to have been able to secure them as translators, "their thorough knowledge of philosophy and their complete command of the German and English languages enabling them to overcome the difficulty of finding adequate English equivalents for the terms of German Philosophy."

Following the publication of the revised German edition in 1918, Professor Hoernlé translated the new passages and other incidental changes that Dr Steiner had made. For this 1922 edition the title was changed, at the author's request, to *The Philosophy of Spiritual Activity*, with the added remark that "throughout the entire work 'freedom' should be taken to mean 'spiritual activity'." The reasons for this change and also for the present decision to change back to the original title are given below (p. xiv).

The translation was revised in 1939 by Dr Hermann Poppelbaum, whose object was to "check certain words and phrases from the strictly Steiner point of view". He wrote in his preface as follows:

> The readers of the German original of this book will know that the author's argument is largely based upon a distinction between the different elements making up the act of Knowledge. English philosophical terms are rarely exact equivalents of German philosophical terms, and the translator's standing problem is to avoid, or at least to minimize, the ambiguities resulting therefrom. The aim of the present revision of the original translation has been to help the reader to understand the analysis of the act of Knowledge and to enable him to follow the subsequent chapters without being troubled by ambiguous terms.

In spite of Dr Poppelbaum's removal of certain ambiguities, readers were still troubled by difficulties that did not derive from the original German. When I was asked by the publishers to prepare this new edition, it soon became clear to me that further alterations to words and phrases would not be sufficient to remove these difficulties. It may therefore be helpful to state briefly what my guiding principles have been in making this translation.

Steiner did not write his book as a thesis for students of philosophy, but in order to give a sound philosophical basis to the experience of oneself as a free spirit—an experience that is open to everybody. The book is written in such a way that the very reading of it is a help towards participating in this experience. For this reason all the terms used must convey a real meaning to the reader, and any explanations required must be in words that are self-evident. Indeed, Steiner states clearly that the terms he uses do not always have the precise meanings given in current scientific writings, but that his intention is to record the facts of everyday experience (see page 20). I have tried throughout to convey the essential meaning of Steiner's original words, and to follow closely his train of thought, so that the English reader may have as nearly as possible the same experience that a German reader has from the original text. Thus the structure of the original has been preserved, sentence by sentence. It might be argued that a "free" translation, making full use of English idiom and style, would be far more appropriate for an English reader; this could cut out the wordy repetitions and lengthy phrases typical of German philosophical writing and make for a more readable text. But it would also have to be written out of the English philosophical tradition, and would require a complete reconstruction of Steiner's arguments from the point of view of an Englishman's philosophy. This might be an excellent thing to do, but would constitute a new work, not a translation. Even if it were attempted, there would still be the need for a close translation making Steiner's path of knowledge available in detail for the English reader.

The method I have followed was to make a fresh translation of each passage and then compare it with the existing one, choosing the better version of the two. Where there was no advantage in making a change, I have left the earlier version, so that many passages appear unaltered from the previous edition. This is therefore a thoroughly revised, rather than an entirely new, translation. It is my hope that it will prove straightforward reading for anyone prepared to follow the author along the path of experience he has described. The following notes explaining certain of the terms used are intended for those who want to compare this edition with the German original, or who are making a special study of philosophy.

FREEDOM is not an exact equivalent of the German word *Freiheit,* although among its wide spectrum of meanings there are some that do correspond. In certain circumstances, however, the differences are important. Steiner himself drew attention to this, for instance, in a lecture he gave at Oxford in 1922, where he said with reference to this book,

> "Therefore today we need above all a view of the world based on *Freiheit*—one can use this word in German, but here in England one must put it differently because the word 'freedom' has a different meaning—one must say a view of the world based on spiritual activity, on action, on thinking and feeling that arise from the individual human spirit." (Translated from the German.)

Steiner also drew attention to the different endings of the words; *Freiheit* could be rendered literally as "freehood" if such a word existed. The German ending *-heit* implied an inner condition or degree, while *-tum*, corresponding to our "-dom", implied something granted or imposed from outside. This is only partly true in English, as a consideration of the words "manhood", "knighthood", "serfdom", "earldom", and "wisdom" will show. In any case, meanings change with time, and current usage rather than etymology is the best guide.

When describing any kind of creative activity we speak of a "freedom of style" or "freedom of expression" in a way that indicates an inner conquest of outer restraints. This inner conquest is the theme of the book, and it is in this sense that I believe the title *The Philosophy of Freedom* would be understood today. When Steiner questioned the aptness of this title, he expressed the view that English people believed that they already possessed freedom, and that they needed to be shocked out of their complacency and made to realize that the freedom he meant had to be attained by hard work. While this may still be true today, the alternative he suggested is now less likely to achieve this shock than is the original. I have not found that the title " The Philosophy of Spiritual Activity" gives the newcomer any indication that the goal of the book is the attainment of inner freedom. Today it is just as likely to suggest a justification of religious practices. Throughout the book it has proved quite impossible to translate *Freiheit* as "spiritual activity" wherever it occurs. The word appears in the titles of the parts of the book and of some of the chapters; the book opens with the question of freedom or necessity, and the final sentence (page 218) is "He is free." Undoubtedly "freedom" is the proper English word to express the main theme of the book, and should also appear in the book's title. Times have changed, and what may well have been good reasons for changing the title in 1922 are not necessarily still valid. After much thought, and taking everything into account, I have decided that the content of the book is better represented today by the title *The Philosophy of Freedom*. Moreover, with this title the book may be instantly identified with *Die Philosophie der Freiheit*, and I have already remarked that this edition is intended as a close translation of the German, rather than a new book specially written for the English.

SPIRIT, SOUL and MIND are not precise equivalents in English of the German *Geist* and *Seele*. Perhaps because we use the concept of mind to include all our experiences through thinking, the concepts of spirit and soul have practically dropped out of everyday use, whereas in German there is no distinct equivalent for "mind" and the concepts "spirit" (*Geist*) and "soul" (*Seele*) are consequently broader in scope. Any work describing Steiner's point of view in terms of English philosophy would have to deal with the mind as a central theme,[5] but here our task is to introduce readers to Steiner's concepts of spirit and soul. For Steiner, the spirit is experienced directly in the act of intuitive thinking. The human spirit is that part of us that thinks, but the spiritual world is not limited to the personal field of the individual human being; it opens out to embrace the eternal truths of existence. The English word "spirit" gives the sense of something more universal, less personal, than "mind", and since Steiner's philosophical path leads to an experience of the reality of the spiritual world, I have kept the word wherever possible, using "mind" or "mental" in a few places where it seemed more appropriate. The "spiritual activity" here meant is thus more than mental activity, although it starts at a level we would call mental; it leads the human being, aware of himself as a spirit, into the ultimate experience of truth.

The soul, too, is directly experienced; it is not a vague metaphysical entity, but is that region in us where we experience our likes and dislikes, our feelings of pleasure and pain. It contains those characteristics of thought and feeling that make us individual, different from each other. In many common phrases we use the word "mind" where German has the word *Seele*, but since Steiner recognizes a distinction between soul and spirit, it is important to keep these different words. Even in modern English usage something of this difference remains, and it is not too late to hope that

[5] See "Rudolf Steiner's Concept of Mind" by Owen Barfield, in *The Faithful Thinker*, pp. 11-21.

Steiner's exact observations in this realm may help to prevent the terms "soul" and "spirit" becoming mere synonyms. Therefore I have kept these words wherever the distinction was important, though in a few places an alternative rendering seemed to fit better; for instance, the "introspective observation" quoted in the motto on the title-page could have been rendered literally as "observation of the soul"—this observation involves a critical examination of our habits of thought and feeling, not studied from *outside* in the manner of a psychological survey of human behaviour, but from *inside* where each person meets himself face to face.

The whole book can be considered as a study of the mind, but using an exactness of observation and clarity of thinking never before achieved. Nevertheless, the stream of materialism still flows so strongly that there is a real danger that the mind, and indeed the whole realm of the soul and the spirit, will be dismissed as a metaphysical construction. Only by adopting a philosophy such as is developed in this book will it be possible to retain an experience of soul and of spirit which will be strong enough to stand up to the overwhelming desire to accept nothing as real unless it is supported by science. For in this philosophy Steiner opens the door to a science of the spirit every bit as exact and precise as our current science of nature would be.

CONCEPT and **PERCEPT** are the direct equivalents of *Begriff* and *Wahrnehmung*. The concept is something grasped by thinking, an element of the world of ideas. Steiner describes what it is at the beginning of Chapter 4 (see page 40).

In describing the percept (see page 44), Steiner mentions the ambiguity of current speech. The German word *Wahrnehmung*, like the English "perception", can mean either the *process* of perceiving or the *object perceived* as an element of observation. Steiner uses the word in the latter sense, and the word "percept", though not perhaps in common use, does avoid the ambiguity. The word does not refer to an actual concrete object that is being observed, for this would only be recognized as such after the appropriate concept had been attached to it, but to the content of observation devoid of any conceptual element. This includes not only sensations of colour, sound, pressure, warmth, taste, smell, and so on, but feelings of pleasure and pain and even thoughts, once the thinking is done. Modern science has come to the conclusion that one cannot deal with a sensation devoid of any conceptual element, and uses the term "perception" to include the whole response to a stimulus, in other words, to mean the *result* of perceiving. But even if one cannot communicate the nature of an experience of pure percept to another person, one must still be able to deal with it as an essential part of the analysis of the process of knowledge. Using the word "percept" for this element of the analysis, we are free to keep the word "perception" for the process of perceiving.

IDEA and MENTAL PICTURE, as used here, correspond to the German words *Idee* and *Vorstellung* respectively. Normally these would both be rendered as "idea", and this practice led to an ambiguity that obscured a distinction central to Steiner's argument. This was the main cause of Dr Poppelbaum's concern, and his solution was to render *Vorstellung* as "representation" and *Idee* as "Idea" with a capital "I". Though this usage may have philosophical justification, it has been my experience in group studies of this book over many years that it has never been fully accepted in practice; "representation" remains a specialist term with a sense rather different from its usual meaning in English, and it certainly does not have the same obvious meaning for the English reader that *Vorstellung* has for the German.

In explaining his use of the word "representation", Dr Poppelbaum wrote in his preface as follows:

> The mental picture which the thinker forms to represent the concept in an individual way is here called a "representation" . . .

Since "mental picture" is here used to explain the term "representation", it seems simpler to use "mental picture" throughout. It fits Steiner's treatment very well, since it conveys to the reader both the sense of something conceptual, in that it is mental, and the sense of something perceptual, in that it is a picture. In fact, Steiner gives two definitions of the mental picture, one as a "percept in my self" (see page 49) and another as an "individualized concept" (see page 84), and it is this intermediate position between percept and concept that gives the mental picture its importance in the process of knowledge.

Another advantage of the term "mental picture" is that the verb "to picture" corresponds well with the German *vorstellen*, implying a mental creation of a scene rather than a physical representation with pencil, paints or camera, which would be "to depict". Of course the visual term "picture" must be understood to cover also the content of other senses, for instance, a remembered tune or a recollection of tranquillity, but this broadening of meaning through analogy is inherent in English usage.

Although mental pictures are commonly regarded as a special

xvii

class of ideas, here the term "idea" is used only for the German *Idee*, without ambiguity. Ideas are not individualized, but are "fuller, more saturated, more comprehensive concepts" (see page 40). In the later part of the book, when discussing the nature of a conscious motive, Steiner uses the word to include all concepts in the most general way, individualized or not, which comes very close to the English use of the word "idea".

IMAGINATION means the faculty and process of creating mental pictures. The word is the same as the German *Imagination*, but I have also used it for the German *Phantasie*, because the word "fantasy" suggests something altogether too far from reality, whereas "imagination" can mean something not only the product of our own consciousness, but also a step towards the realization of something new. Thus the title given to Chapter 12, Moral Imagination (for *Moralische Phantasie*), seemed to me to be correct, and I have kept it. It describes the process of taking an abstract idea, or concept, and creating a vivid mental picture of how it can be applied in a particular circumstance, so that it may become the motive for a moral deed.

In later writings Steiner describes how this ordinary faculty of imagining, or making mental pictures, can be developed to the point where it becomes the faculty of actually perceiving the creative ideas behind the phenomena of nature. In these later writings "Imagination" becomes a special term to indicate this level of perception, but in this book the meaning remains near to the ordinary usage. However, the gateway to such higher levels of perception is opened through the path of experience here set forth.

INTUITION is again the same as the German word, and means the faculty and process of grasping concepts, in particular the immediate apprehension of a thought without reasoning. This is the normal English usage, though Steiner uses the term in an exact way, as follows (see page 73):

> In contrast to the content of the percept which is given to us from without, the content of thinking appears inwardly. The form in which this first makes its appearance we will call *intuition*. *Intuition* is for thinking what *observation* is for the percept.

Later in the book he gives another definition (see page 122):

> Intuition is the conscious experience—in pure spirit—of a purely spiritual content. Only through an intuition can the essence of thinking be grasped.

From this it is not difficult to see how again, in later writings, Steiner could describe a stage of perception still higher than that called "Imagination", the stage of "Intuition" in which one immediately apprehends the reality of other spiritual beings. Although this book deals only with the spiritual content of pure thinking, intuition at this level is also a step towards a higher level of perceiving reality.

EXPERIENCE has two meanings, which correspond to different words in German. "Actual observation of facts or events" corresponds to the German *Erlebnis* and to the verb *erleben*, while "the knowledge resulting from this observation" corresponds to *Erfahrung*. Thus the accumulation of knowledge can be described as "past experience" or "total sum of experience", if the single word is ambiguous (see, for instance, page 85). When speaking of human behaviour that is based on past experience, Steiner calls it *praktische Erfahrung*, which is rendered as "practical experience" (see page 128).

On the other hand, having direct experience as an activity of observation is expressed by the verb *erleben*, which means literally "to live through". Thus, in the latter part of the book, particularly in those passages which were added in 1918 (see pages 107 and 219-220), Steiner speaks repeatedly of the "thinking which can be experienced". This experience is to be understood as every bit as real and concrete as the "actual observation of facts and events" described above.

MOTIVE and **DRIVING FORCE** are two elements in any act of will that have to be recognized as distinct (see page 124). They correspond to the German words *Motiv* and *Triebfeder*, respectively.

"Motive", as used by Steiner, corresponds exactly to the common English usage, meaning the reason that a person has for his action. It has to be a conscious motive, in the form of a concept or mental picture, or else we cannot speak of an act of will, let alone a moral deed. An "unconscious motive" is really a contradiction in terms, and should properly be described as a driving force—it implies that some other person has been able to grasp the concept which was the reason for the action, though the person acting was not himself aware of it; he acted as an automaton, or, as we properly say, "without motive". Nevertheless, modern psychology has contrived to define the "motive" as something no different from the driving force, which precludes the recognition of a motive grasped out of pure intuition, and therefore of the essential difference between a moral deed where a man knows why he acts and an amoral one where his knowledge is a matter of indifference. By making the distinction between motive and driving force, Steiner has been able to characterize all possible levels of action from the purely instinctive to the completely free deed.

The literal meaning of *Triebfeder* is the mainspring that drives a piece of clockwork. In previous editions, this was rendered as "spring of action". While this is legitimate philosophical usage, I found that it was often misunderstood by the ordinary reader, being taken to mean a spring like a fountain or river-source, as in the phrase "springs of life". This immediately causes confusion with the origin or source of the action, which is the motive. Of course, at the higher levels of action there is no other driving force than the idea which stands as the motive, but in order to follow the development from lower levels one must distinguish the idea, which is the motive, from whatever it is in us that throws us into action whenever a suitable motive presents itself. "Mainspring" does not always fit well in the text, and after trying various words and phrases I have chosen "driving force" as best expressing the dynamic nature of this part of our constitution. The driving force differs from the motive in that we may well remain unconscious of it. But if we are not conscious of the driving force behind our actions, we cannot be acting in freedom, even though we are aware of our motives. Only if we make our own ideals the driving force of our will can we act in freedom, because then nothing apart from ourselves determines our action. Thus the final triumph of Steiner's path of development depends on making this clear distinction between motive and driving force. A view that treats all motives as driving forces will not be able to recognize the possibility of freedom, while a view that regards all driving forces as ideal elements will not see the need for overcoming our unconscious urges and habits if freedom is to be attained.

WILL and **WANT** are two distinct words in English where the German has only one verb *wollen* and its derivatives. Here the task of translating runs into a considerable difficulty, for in any discussion of free will it is important to be clear what willing is. The noun forms are fairly straightforward: *ein Wollen* means "an act of will", *das Wollen* means "willing" in general, and *der Wille* means "the will". But the English verb "to will" has a restricted range of meaning, and to use it all the time to render the German *wollen* can be quite misleading. An example is the quotation from Hamerling in the first chapter (see page 9):

> *Der Mensch kann allerdings tun, was er will—aber er kann nicht wollen, was er will, weil sein Wille durch Motive bestimmt ist.*

The previous edition rendered this:

> Man can, it is true, do what he wills, but he cannot will what he wills, because his will is determined by motives.

If this means anything at all in English, it means that man cannot direct his will as he chooses. The archaic sense of "willing" as "desiring" is kept in the phrase "what he wills", in keeping with current usage, for instance, in the remark "Come when you will." But the active sense of "willing" as contrasted with "doing" implies a metaphysical power of compulsion quite out of keeping with Steiner's whole method of treating the subject. This metaphysical attitude to the will is clearly expressed in a sentence such as "I willed him to go", which implies something more than mere desire but less than overt action. It is less obvious when dealing with the genesis of one's own actions, but the tendency to attribute a metaphysical quality to the will is developed in Schopenhauer's philosophy, and this may well be a tendency inherent in the German language. Steiner has no such intention, and he leaves us in no doubt that his use of *wollen* implies a definite element of desire (see page 198); indeed, the highest expression of man's will is when it becomes the faculty of spiritual desire or craving (*geistige Begehrungsvermögen*). Therefore, whenever the archaic sense of the verb "to will" is not appropriate, I have decided that it is better to render the German verb *wollen* with the English "want" and its variants, "wanting", "to want to . . ." and so on. This makes immediate good sense of many passages, and moreover if one would translate this back into German one would have to use the word *wollen*. Hamerling's sentence now becomes:

> Man can certainly do as he wills, but he cannot want as he wills, because his wanting is determined by motives.

Although Steiner has to show that this view is mistaken, one can at least understand how it could come to be written. That it can be a genuine human experience is shown by the similar remark attributed to T. E. Lawrence, "I can do what I want, but I cannot want what I want." In other words, "I can carry out any desires for action that I may have, but I cannot choose how these desires come to me." Both Lawrence and Hamerling leave out of account just

xxi

those cases where man *can* want as he wills, because he has freely chosen his own motive. Steiner's treatment of the will overcomes any necessity for metaphysical thinking; for instance, it now makes sense to say that to want without motive would make the will an "empty faculty" (see page 9), because to want without wanting *something* would be meaningless.

I have dealt with this at some length because it has been my experience that the message of the entire book springs to life in a new and vivid way when it is realized that the original motive power of the will is in fact *desire*, and that desire can be transformed by knowledge into its most noble form, which is *love*.

* * *

It was the late Friedrich Geuter who showed me, together with many others, the importance of this book as a basis for the social as well as the intellectual life of today. My debt to the previous translators and editors will already be clear. I also owe much to the many friends who have taken part in joint studies of this book over the past thirty years and to those who have helped and advised me with suggestions for the translation, especially the late George Adams, Owen Barfield, and Rita Stebbing. Finally I must mention my colleague Ralph Brocklebank, who has shared much of the work, and, with Dorothy Osmond, prepared it for the Press.

Michael Wilson, Clent, 1964.

AUTHOR'S PREFACES

Preface to the revised edition of 1918

There are two fundamental questions in the life of the human soul towards which everything to be discussed in this book is directed. One is: Is it possible to find a view of the essential nature of man such as will give us a foundation for everything else that comes to meet us—whether through life experience or through science—which we feel is otherwise not self-supporting and therefore liable to be driven by doubt and criticism into the realm of uncertainty? The other question is this: Is man entitled to claim for himself freedom of will, or is freedom a mere illusion begotten of his inability to recognize the threads of necessity on which his will, like any natural event, depends? It is no artificial tissue of theories that provokes this question. In a certain mood it presents itself quite naturally to the human soul. And one may well feel that if the soul has not at some time found itself faced in utmost seriousness by the problem of free will or necessity it will not have reached its full stature. This book is intended to show that the experiences which the second problem causes man's soul to undergo depend upon the position he is able to take up towards the first problem. An attempt is made to prove that there *is* a view of the nature of man's being which can support the rest of knowledge; and further, that this view completely justifies the idea of free will, provided only that we have first discovered that region of the soul in which free will can unfold itself.

The view to which we here refer is one which, once gained, is capable of becoming part and parcel of the very life of the soul itself. The answer given to the two problems will not be of the purely theoretical sort which, once mastered, may be carried about as a conviction preserved by memory. Such an answer would, for the whole manner of thinking on which this book is based, be no real answer at all. The book will not give a ready-made self-contained answer of this sort, but will point to a field of experience in which man's inner soul activity supplies a living answer to these questions at every moment that he needs one. Whoever has once discovered the region of the soul where these questions unfold, will find that the very contemplation of this region gives him all that he needs for the solution of the two problems. With the knowledge thus acquired, he may then, as desire or destiny impels him, adventure further into the breadths and depths of this enigmatical life of ours. Thus it would appear that a kind of knowledge which proves its justification and validity by its own inner life as well as by the kinship of its own life with the whole life of the human soul, does in fact exist.

This is how I thought about the content of this book when I first wrote it down twenty-five years ago. Today, once again, I have to set down similar sentences if I am to characterize the main ideas of the book. At the original writing I limited myself to saying no more than was in the strictest sense connected with the two fundamental questions which I have outlined. If anyone should be astonished at not finding in this book any reference to that region of the world of spiritual experience described in my later writings, I would ask him to bear in mind that it was not my purpose at that time to set down the results of spiritual research, but first to lay the foundations on which such results can rest.

The Philosophy of Freedom does not contain any results of this sort, any more than it contains special results of the natural sciences. But what it does contain is in my judgment absolutely necessary for anyone who seeks a secure foundation for such knowledge. What I have said in this book may be acceptable even to some who, for reasons of their own, refuse to have anything to do with the results of my researches into the spiritual realm. But anyone who feels drawn towards the results of these spiritual researches may well appreciate the importance of what I was here trying to do. It is this: to show that open-minded consideration simply of the two questions I have indicated and which are fundamental for every kind of knowledge, leads to the view that man lives in the midst of a genuine spiritual world.

In this book the attempt is made to show that a knowledge of the spirit realm *before* entering upon actual spiritual experience is fully justified. The course of this demonstration is so conducted that for anyone who is able and willing to enter into these arguments it is never necessary, in order to accept them, to cast furtive glances at the experiences which my later writings have shown to be relevant.

Thus it seems to me that in one sense this book occupies a position completely independent of my writings on actual spiritual scientific matters. Yet in another sense it is most intimately connected with them. These considerations have moved me now, after a lapse of twenty-five years, to republish the contents of this book practically unaltered in all essentials. I have, however, made additions of some length to a number of chapters. The misunderstandings of my argument which I have met seemed to make these more detailed elaborations necessary. Changes of text have been made only where it appeared to me that I had said clumsily what I meant to say a quarter of a century ago. (Only ill will could find in these changes occasion to suggest that I have changed my fundamental conviction.)

For many years my book has been out of print. In spite of the fact, which is apparent from what I have just said, that my utterances of twenty-five years ago about these problems still seem to me just as relevant today, I hesitated a long time about the completion of this revised edition. Again and again I have asked myself whether I ought not, at this point or that, to define my position towards the numerous philosophical views which have been put forward since the publication of the first edition. Yet my preoccupation in recent years with researches into the purely spiritual realm prevented me from doing this in the way I could have wished. However, a survey of the philosophical literature of the present day, as thorough as I could make it, has convinced me that such a critical discussion, tempting though it would be in itself, would be out of place in the context of this book. All that it seemed to me necessary to say about recent philosophical tendencies, from the point of view of the *Philosophy of Freedom*, may be found in the second volume of my *Riddles of Philosophy*.

Rudolf Steiner, April 1918.

Preface to the first edition, 1894; revised, 1918

In the following is reproduced, in all essentials, what stood as a preface in the first edition of this book. Since it shows the mood of thought out of which I wrote this book twenty-five years ago, rather than having any direct bearing on its contents, I include it here as an appendix. I do not want to omit it altogether, because the opinion keeps cropping up that I need to suppress some of my earlier writings on account of my later ones on spiritual science. Only the very first introductory sentences of this preface (in the first edition) have been altogether omitted here, because today they seem to me quite irrelevant. But the rest of what was said seems to me necessary even today, in spite of, indeed, just because of the natural scientific manner of thinking of our contemporaries.

Our age can only accept *truth* from the depths of human nature. Of Schiller's two well-known paths, it is the second that will mostly be chosen at the present time:

Truth seek we both—Thou in the life without thee and around;
I in the heart within. By both can Truth alike be found.
The healthy eye can through the world the great Creator track;
The healthy heart is but the glass which gives Creation back.

(Translation by E. Bulwer Lytton.)

A truth which comes to us from outside always bears the stamp of uncertainty. We can believe only what appears to each one of us in our own hearts as truth.

Only the truth can give us assurance in developing our individual powers. Whoever is tortured by doubts finds his powers lamed. In a world full of riddles, he can find no goal for his creative energies.

We no longer want merely to *believe*; we want to *know*. Belief demands the acceptance of truths which we do not fully comprehend. But things we do not fully comprehend are repugnant to the individual element in us, which wants to experience everything in the depths of its inner being. The only *knowledge* which satisfies us is one which is subject to no external standards but springs from the inner life of the personality.

Again, we do not want any knowledge of the kind that has become frozen once and for all into rigid academic rules, preserved in encyclopaedias valid for all time. Each of us claims the right to start from the facts that lie nearest to hand, from his own immediate experiences, and thence to ascend to a knowledge of the whole universe. We strive after certainty in knowledge, but each in his own way.

Our scientific doctrines, too, should no longer be formulated as if we were unconditionally compelled to accept them. None of us would wish to give a scientific work a title like Fichte's "A Pellucid Account for the General Public concerning the Real Nature of the Newest Philosophy. *An Attempt to Compel the Readers to Understand.*" Today nobody should be *compelled* to understand. From anyone who is not driven to a certain view by his own individual needs, we demand no acknowledgement or agreement. Even with the immature human being, the child, we do not nowadays cram knowledge into it, but we try to develop its capacities so that it will no longer need to be *compelled* to understand, but will *want* to understand.

I am under no illusion about these characteristics of my time. I know how much the tendency prevails to make things impersonal and stereotyped. But I know equally well that many of my contemporaries try to order their lives in the kind of way I have indicated. To them I would dedicate this book.

It is not meant to give "the only possible" path to the truth, but is meant to *describe* the path taken by one for whom truth is the main concern.

The book leads at first into somewhat abstract regions, where thought must draw sharp outlines if it is to reach clearly defined positions. But the reader will also be led out of these arid concepts into concrete life. I am indeed fully convinced that one must raise oneself into the ethereal realm of concepts if one would experience every aspect of existence. Whoever appreciates only the pleasures of the senses is unacquainted with life's sweetest savours. The oriental sages make their disciples live a life of renunciation and asceticism for years before they impart to them their own wisdom. The western world no longer demands pious exercises and ascetic habits as a preparation for science, but it does require the willingness to withdraw oneself awhile from the immediate impressions of life, and to betake oneself into the realm of pure thought.

The realms of life are many. For each one, special sciences develop. But life itself is a unity, and the more deeply the sciences try to penetrate into their separate realms, the more they withdraw themselves from the vision of the world as a living whole. There must be a knowledge which seeks in the separate sciences the elements for leading man back once more to the fullness of life. The scientific specialist seeks through his findings to develop awareness of the world and its workings; in this book the aim is a philosophical one— that knowledge itself shall become organically alive. The separate sciences are stages on the way to that knowledge we are here trying to achieve. A similar relationship exists in the arts. The composer works on the basis of the theory of composition. This theory is a collection of rules which one has to know in order to compose. In composing, the rules of the theory become the servants of life itself, of reality. In exactly the same sense, philosophy is an *art*. All real philosophers have been *artists in the realm of concepts*. For them, human ideas were their artists' materials and scientific method their artistic technique. Abstract thinking thus takes on concrete individual life. The ideas become powerful forces in life. Then we do not merely have knowledge about things, but have made knowledge into a real self-governing organism; our actual working consciousness has risen beyond a mere passive reception of truths.

How philosophy as an art is related to human *freedom*, what freedom is, and whether we do, or can, participate in it—this is the main theme of my book. All other scientific discussions are included only because they ultimately throw light on these questions, which are, in my opinion, the most immediate concern of mankind. These pages offer a *"Philosophy of Freedom"*.

All science would be nothing but the satisfaction of idle curiosity did it not strive to raise the *value of existence for the personality of man*. The sciences attain their true value only by showing the human significance of their results. The ultimate aim of the individual can never be the cultivation of a single faculty, but only the development of all the capacities that slumber within us. Knowledge has value only in so far as it contributes to the *all-round* development of the *whole* nature of man.

This book, therefore, conceives the relationship between science and life, not in such a way that man must bow down before an idea and devote his powers to its service, but in the sense that he masters the world of ideas in order to use them for his *human* aims, which transcend those of mere science.

One must be able to confront an idea and experience it; otherwise one will fall into its bondage.

KNOWLEDGE OF FREEDOM

CHAPTER ONE

Conscious Human Action

Is man in his thinking and acting a spiritually *free* being, or is he compelled by the iron necessity of purely natural law? There are few questions upon which so much sagacity has been brought to bear. The idea of the freedom of the human will has found enthusiastic supporters and stubborn opponents in plenty. There are those who, in their moral fervour, label anyone a man of limited intelligence who can deny so patent a *fact* as freedom. Opposed to them are others who regard it as the acme of unscientific thinking for anyone to believe that the uniformity of natural law is broken in the sphere of human action and thinking. One and the same thing is thus proclaimed, now as the most precious possession of humanity, now as its most fatal illusion. Infinite subtlety has been employed to explain how human freedom can be consistent with the laws working in nature, of which man, after all, is a part. No less is the trouble to which others have gone to explain how such a delusion as this could have arisen. That we are dealing here with one of the most important questions for life, religion, conduct, science, must be felt by anyone who includes any degree of thoroughness at all in his make-up. It is one of the sad signs of the superficiality of present-day thought that a book which attempts to develop a new faith out of the results of recent scientific research,* has nothing more to say on this question than these words:

> With the question of the freedom of the human will we are not concerned. The alleged freedom of indifferent choice has

* David Friedrich Strauss, *Der alte und neue Glaube.*

3

been recognized as an empty illusion by every philosophy worthy of the name. The moral valuation of human action and character remains untouched by this problem.

It is not because I consider that the book in which it occurs has any special importance that I quote this passage, but because it seems to me to express the view to which the thinking of most of our contemporaries manages to rise in this matter. Everyone who claims to have grown beyond the kindergarten stage of science appears to know nowadays that freedom cannot consist in choosing, at one's pleasure, one or other of two possible courses of action. There is always, so we are told, a perfectly definite *reason* why, out of several possible actions, we carry out just one and no other.

This seems obvious. Nevertheless, down to the present day, the main attacks of the opponents of freedom are directed only against freedom of choice. Even Herbert Spencer, whose doctrines are gaining ground daily, says,

> *That everyone is at liberty to desire or not to desire*, which is the real proposition involved in the dogma of free will, is negatived as much by the analysis of consciousness, as by the contents of the preceding chapter.*

Others, too, start from the same point of view in combating the concept of free will. The germs of all the relevant arguments are to be found as early as Spinoza. All that he brought forward in clear and simple language against the idea of freedom has since been repeated times without number, but as a rule enveloped in the most hair-splitting theoretical doctrines, so that it is difficult to recognize the straightforward train of thought which is all that matters. Spinoza writes in a letter of October or November, 1674,

* *The Principles of Psychology*, 1855, German edition 1882; Part IV, Chap. ix, par. 219.

I call a thing *free* which exists and acts from the pure necessity of its nature, and I call that *unfree*, of which the being and action are precisely and fixedly determined by something else. Thus, for example, God, though necessary, is free because he exists only through the necessity of his own nature. Similarly, God cognizes himself and all else freely, because it follows solely from the necessity of his nature that he cognizes all. You see, therefore, that for me freedom consists not in free decision, but in free necessity.

But let us come down to created things which are all determined by external causes to exist and to act in a fixed and definite manner. To perceive this more clearly, let us imagine a perfectly simple case. A stone, for example, receives from an external cause acting upon it a certain quantity of motion, by reason of which it necessarily continues to move, after the impact of the external cause has ceased. The continued motion of the stone is due to compulsion, not to the necessity of its own nature, because it requires to be defined by the thrust of an external cause. What is true here for the stone is true also for every other particular thing, however complicated and many-sided it may be, namely, that everything is necessarily determined by external causes to exist and to act in a fixed and definite manner.

Now, please, suppose that this stone during its motion thinks and knows that it is striving to the best of its ability to continue in motion. This stone, which is conscious only of its striving and is by no means indifferent, will believe that it is absolutely free, and that it continues in motion for no other reason than its own will to continue. But this is just the human freedom that everybody claims to possess and which consists in nothing but this, that men are conscious of their desires, but ignorant of the causes by which they are determined. Thus the child believes that he desires milk of his own free will, the angry boy regards his desire for vengeance as free, and the coward his desire for flight. Again, the drunken man believes that he says of his own free will what, sober

5

again, he would fain have left unsaid, and as this prejudice is innate in all men, it is difficult to free oneself from it. For, although experience teaches us often enough that man least of all can temper his desires, and that, moved by conflicting passions, he sees the better and pursues the worse, yet he considers himself free because there are some things which he desires less strongly, and some desires which he can easily inhibit through the recollection of something else which it is often possible to recall.

Because this view is so clearly and definitely ex pressed it is easy to detect the fundamental error that it contains. The same necessity by which a stone makes a definite movement as the result of an impact, is said to compel a man to carry out an action when impelled thereto by any reason. It is only because man is conscious of his action that he thinks himself to be its originator. But in doing so he overlooks the fact that he is driven by a cause which he cannot help obeying. The error in this train of thought is soon discovered. Spinoza, and all who think like him, overlook the fact that man not only is conscious of his action, but also may become conscious of the causes which guide him. Nobody will deny that the child is *unfree* when he desires milk, or the drunken man when he says things which he later regrets. Neither knows anything of the causes, working in the depths of their organisms, which exercise irresistible control over them. But is it justifiable to lump together actions of this kind with those in which a man is conscious not only of his actions but also of the reasons which cause him to act? Are the actions of men really all of one kind? Should the act of a soldier on the field of battle, of the scientific researcher in his laboratory, of the statesman in the most complicated diplomatic negotiations, be placed scientifically on the same level with that of the child when it desires milk? It is no doubt true that it is

6

best to seek the solution of a problem where the conditions are simplest. But inability to discriminate has before now caused endless confusion. There is, after all, a profound difference between knowing why I am acting and not knowing it. At first sight this seems a self-evident truth. And yet the opponents of freedom never ask themselves whether a motive of action which I recognize and see through, is to be regarded as compulsory for me in the same sense as the organic process which causes the child to cry for milk.

Eduard von Hartmann asserts that the human will depends on two chief factors, the motives and the character.* If one regards men as all alike, or at any rate the differences between them as negligible, then their will appears as determined from *without*, that is to say, by the circumstances which come to meet them. But if one bears in mind that a man adopts an idea, or mental picture, as the motive of his action only if his character is such that this mental picture arouses a desire in him, then he appears as determined from *within* and not from *without*. Now because, in accordance with his character, he must first adopt as a motive a mental picture given to him from without, a man believes he is free, that is, independent of external impluses. The truth, however, according to Eduard von Hartmann, is that

> even though we ourselves first adopt a mental picture as a motive, we do so not arbitrarily, but according to the necessity of our characterological disposition, that is, we are *anything but free.*

Here again the difference between motives which I allow to influence me only after I have permeated them with my consciousness, and those which I follow without any clear knowledge of them, is absolutely ignored.

This leads us straight to the standpoint from which the

* *Phaenomenologie des sittlichen Bewusstseins*, p. 451.

7

subject will be considered here. Have we any right to consider the question of the freedom of the will by itself at all? And if not, with what other question must it necessarily be connected?

If there is a difference between a conscious motive of action and an unconscious urge, then the conscious motive will result in an action which must be judged differently from one that springs from blind impluse. Hence our first question will concern this difference, and on the result of this enquiry will depend what attitude we shall have to take towards the question of freedom proper.

What does it mean to have *knowledge* of the reasons for one's action? Too little attention has been paid to this question because, unfortunately, we have torn into two what is really an inseparable whole: Man. We have distinguished between the knower and the doer and have left out of account precisely the one who matters most of all—*the knowing doer.*

It is said that man is free when he is controlled only by his reason and not by his animal passions. Or again, that to be free means to be able to determine one's life and action by purposes and deliberate decisions.

Nothing is gained by assertions of this sort. For the question is just whether reason, purposes, and decisions exercise the same kind of compulsion over a man as his animal passions. If without my co-operation, a rational decision emerges in me with the same necessity with which hunger and thirst arise, then I must needs obey it, and my freedom is an illusion.

Another form of expression runs: to be free does not mean to be able to *want* as one wills, but to be able to *do* as one wills. This thought has been expressed with great clearness by the poet-philosopher Robert Hamerling.

Man can certainly do as he wills, but he cannot want as he wills, because his wanting is determined by *motives*. He cannot want as he wills? Let us consider these phrases more closely. Have they any intelligible meaning? Freedom of will would then mean being able to want without ground, without motive. But what does wanting mean if not *to have grounds* for doing, or trying to do, this rather than that? To want something without ground or motive would be to want something *without wanting it*. The concept of wanting cannot be divorced from the concept of motive. Without a determining motive the will is an empty *faculty*; only through the motive does it become active and real. It is, therefore, quite true that the human will is not "free" inasmuch as its direction is always determined by the strongest motive. But on the other hand it must be admitted that it is absurd, in contrast with this "unfreedom", to speak of a conceivable freedom of the will which would consist in being able to want what one does *not* want.*

Here again, only motives in general are mentioned, without taking into account the difference between unconscious and conscious motives. If a motive affects me, and I am compelled to act on it because it proves to be the "strongest" of its kind, then the thought of freedom ceases to have any meaning. How should it matter to me whether I can do a thing or not, if I am *forced* by the motive to do it? The primary question is not whether I can do a thing or not when a motive has worked upon me, but whether there are any motives except such as impel me with absolute necessity. If I am *compelled* to want something, then I may well be absolutely indifferent as to whether I can also do it. And if, through my character, or through circumstances prevailing in my environment, a motive is forced on me which to my thinking is unreasonable, then I should even have to be glad if I could not do what I want.

* *Atomistik des Willens*, Vol. 2, p. 213 ff.

9

The question is not whether I can carry out a decision once made, but *how the decision comes about within me.*

What distinguishes man from all other organic beings arises from his rational thinking. Activity he has in common with other organisms. Nothing is gained by seeking analogies in the animal world to clarify the concept of freedom as applied to the actions of human beings. Modern science loves such analogies. When scientists have succeeded in finding among animals something similar to human behaviour, they believe they have touched on the most important question of the science of man. To what misunderstandings this view leads is seen, for example, in the book *The Illusion of Freewill,* by P. Rée, where the following remark on freedom appears:

> It is easy to explain why the movement of a stone seems to us necessary, while the volition of a donkey does not. The causes which set the stone in motion are external and visible, while the causes which determine the donkey's volition are internal and invisible. Between us and the place of their activity there is the skull of the ass. . . . The determining causes are not visible and therefore thought to be non-existent. The volition, it is explained, is, indeed, the cause of the donkey's turning round, but is itself unconditioned; it is an absolute beginning.*

Here again human actions in which there is a consciousness of the motives are simply ignored, for Rée declares that "between us and the place of their activity there is the skull of the ass." To judge from these words, it has not dawned on Rée that there are actions, not indeed of the ass, but of human beings, in which between us and the action lies the motive *that has become conscious.* Rée demonstrates his blindness once again, a few pages further on, when he says,

> We do not perceive the *causes* by which our will is determined, hence we think it is not causally determined at all.

* *Die Illusion der Willensfreiheit,* 1885, page 5.

But enough of examples which prove that many argue against freedom without knowing in the least what freedom is.

That an action, of which the agent does not know why he performs it, cannot be *free*, goes without saying. But what about an action for which the reasons are known? This leads us to the question of the origin and meaning of thinking. For without the recognition of the *thinking* activity of the soul, it is impossible to form a concept of knowledge *about anything*, and therefore of knowledge about an action. When we know what thinking in general means, it will be easy to get clear about the role that thinking plays in human action. As Hegel rightly says,

> It is thinking that turns the soul, which the animals also possess, into spirit.

Hence it will also be thinking that gives to human action its characteristic stamp.

On no account should it be said that all our action springs only from the sober deliberations of our reason. I am very far from calling *human* in the highest sense only those actions that proceed from abstract judgment. But as soon as our conduct rises above the sphere of the satisfaction of purely animal desires, our motives are always permeated by thoughts. Love, pity, and patriotism are driving forces for actions which cannot be analysed away into cold concepts of the intellect. It is said that here the heart, the mood of the soul, hold sway. No doubt. But the heart and the mood of the soul do not create the motives. They presuppose them and let them enter. Pity enters my heart when the mental picture of a person who arouses pity appears in my consciousness. The way to the heart is through the head. Love is no exception. Whenever it is not merely the expression of bare sexual instinct, it depends on the mental picture we form of the loved one. And the more idealistic these mental pictures are, just so much the more blessed is our love. Here too, thought is the father of feeling. It is said that love makes us blind to the failings of the loved one. But this can be expressed the other way round, namely, that it is just for the good qualities that love opens the eyes. Many pass by these good qualities without noticing them. One, however, perceives them, and just because he does, love awakens in his soul. What else has he done but made a mental picture of what hundreds have failed to see? Love is not theirs, because they lack the *mental picture*.

However we approach the matter, it becomes more and more clear that the question of the nature of human action presupposes that of the origin of thinking. I shall, therefore, turn next to this question.

CHAPTER TWO

The Fundamental Desire for Knowledge

Two souls reside, alas, within my breast,
And each one from the other would be parted.
The one holds fast, in sturdy lust for love,
With clutching organs clinging to the world;
The other strongly rises from the gloom
To lofty fields of ancient heritage.

FAUST I, Scene 2, lines 1112-1117.

In these words Goethe expresses a characteristic feature which is deeply rooted in human nature. Man is not organized as a self-consistent unity. He always demands more than the world, of its own accord, gives him. Nature has endowed us with needs; among them are some that she leaves to our own activity to satisfy. Abundant as are the gifts she has bestowed upon us, still more abundant are our desires. We seem born to be dissatisfied. And our thirst for knowledge is but a special instance of this dissatisfaction. We look twice at a tree. The first time we see its branches at rest, the second time in motion. We are not satisfied with this observation. Why, we ask, does the tree appear to us now at rest, now in motion? Every glance at Nature evokes in us a multitude of questions. Every phenomenon we meet sets us a new problem. Every experience is a riddle. We see that from the egg there emerges a creature like the mother animal, and we ask the reason for the likeness. We observe a living being grow and develop to a certain degree of perfection, and we seek the underlying conditions for this experience. Nowhere are we satisfied with what Nature spreads out before our senses.

13

Everywhere we seek what we call the *explanation* of the facts.

The something more which we seek in things, over and above what is immediately given to us in them, splits our whole being into two parts. We become conscious of our antithesis to the world. We confront the world as independent beings. The universe appears to us in two opposite parts: *I* and *World*.

We erect this barrier between ourselves and the world as soon as consciousness first dawns in us. But we never cease to feel that, in spite of all, we belong to the world, that there is a connecting link between it and us, and that we are beings within, and not *without*, the universe.

This feeling makes us strive to bridge over this antithesis, and in this bridging lies ultimately the whole spiritual striving of mankind. The history of our spiritual life is a continuing search for the unity between ourselves and the world. Religion, art and science follow, one and all, this aim. The religious believer seeks in the revelation which God grants him the solution to the universal riddle which his I, dissatisfied with the world of mere appearance, sets before him. The artist seeks to embody in his material the ideas that are in his I, in order to reconcile what lives in him with the world outside. He too feels dissatisfied with the world of mere appearance and seeks to mould into it that something more which his I, transcending it, contains. The thinker seeks the laws of phenomena, and strives to penetrate by thinking what he experiences by observing.
•Only when we have made the *world-content* into our *thought-content* do we again find the unity out of which we had separated ourselves. We shall see later that this goal can be reached only if the task of the research scientist is conceived at a much deeper level than is often the case. The whole

situation I have described here presents itself to us on the stage of history in the conflict between the one-world theory, or *monism*, and the two-world theory, or *dualism*.

Dualism pays attention only to the *separation* between I and World which the consciousness of man has brought about. All its efforts consist in a vain struggle to reconcile these opposites, which it calls now *spirit* and *matter*, now *subject* and *object*, now *thinking* and *appearance*. It feels that there must be a bridge between the two worlds but is not in a position to find it. In that man is aware of himself as "I", he cannot but think of this "I" as being on the side of the *spirit*; and in contrasting this "I" with the world, he is bound to put on the world's side the realm of percepts given to the senses, that is, the world of *matter*. In doing so, man puts himself right into the middle of this antithesis of spirit and matter. He is the more compelled to do so because his own body belongs to the material world. Thus the "I", or Ego, belongs to the realm of spirit as a part of it; the *material* objects and events which are perceived by the senses belong to the "World". All the riddles which relate to spirit and matter, man must inevitably rediscover in the fundamental riddle of his own nature.

Monism pays attention only to the unity and tries either to deny or to slur over the opposites, present though they are. Neither of these two points of view can satisfy us, for they do not do justice to the facts. Dualism sees in spirit (I) and matter (World) two fundamentally different entities, and cannot, therefore, understand how they can interact with one another. How should spirit be aware of what goes on in matter, seeing that the essential nature of matter is quite alien to spirit? Or how in these circumstances should spirit act upon matter, so as to translate its intentions into actions? The most ingenious and the most absurd hypotheses have been propounded to answer these questions. Up to the present, however, monism is not in a much better position. It has tried three different ways of meeting the difficulty. Either it denies spirit and becomes materialism; or it denies matter in order to seek its salvation in spiritualism*; or it asserts that even in the simplest entities in the world, spirit and matter are indissolubly bound together so that there is no need to marvel at the appearance in man of these two modes of existence, seeing that they are never found apart.

Materialism can never offer a satisfactory explanation of the world. For every attempt at an explanation must begin with the formation of *thoughts* about the phenomena of the world. Materialism thus begins with the *thought* of matter or material processes. But, in doing so, it is already confronted by two different sets of facts: the material world, and the thoughts about it. The materialist seeks to make these latter intelligible by regarding them as purely material processes. He believes that thinking takes place in the brain, much in the same way that digestion takes place in the animal organs. Just as he attributes mechanical and organic effects to matter, so he credits matter in certain circumstances with the capacity to think. He overlooks that, in doing so, he is merely shifting the problem from one place to another. He ascribes the power of thinking to matter instead of to himself. And thus he is back again at his starting point. How does matter come to think about its own nature? Why is it not simply satisfied with itself and content just to exist? The materialist has turned his attention away from the definite subject, his own I, and has arrived at an image of something quite vague and indefinite. Here the old riddle meets him

* The author refers to philosophical "spiritualism" as opposed to philosophical "materialism". See reference to Fichte that follows (page 17).—*Translator's Footnote.*

again. The materialistic conception cannot solve the problem; it can only shift it from one place to another.

What of the spiritualistic theory? The genuine *spiritualist* denies to matter all independent existence and regards it merely as a product of spirit. But when he tries to use this theory to solve the riddle of his own human nature, he finds himself driven into a corner. Over against the "I" or Ego, which can be ranged on the side of spirit, there stands directly the world of the senses. No *spiritual* approach to it seems open. Only with the help of material processes can it be perceived and experienced by the "I". Such material processes the "I" does not discover in itself so long as it regards its own nature as exclusively spiritual. In what it achieves spiritually by its own effort, the sense-perceptible world is never to be found. It seems as if the "I" had to concede that the world would be a closed book to it unless it could establish a non-spiritual relation to the world. Similarly, when it comes to action, we have to translate our purposes into realities with the help of material things and forces. We are, therefore, referred back to the outer world. The most extreme spiritualist—or rather, the thinker who through his absolute idealism appears as extreme spiritualist—is Johann Gottlieb Fichte. He attempts to derive the whole edifice of the world from the "I". What he has actually accomplished is a magnificent *thought-picture* of the world, without any content of experience. As little as it is possible for the materialist to argue the spirit away, just as little is it possible for the spiritualist to argue away the outer world of matter.

When man reflects upon the "I", he perceives in the first instance the work of this "I" in the conceptual elaboration of the world of ideas. Hence a world-conception that inclines towards spiritualism may feel tempted, in looking at man's own essential nature, to acknowledge nothing of spirit except this world of ideas. In this way spiritualism becomes one-sided idealism. Instead of going on to penetrate *through* the world of ideas to the *spiritual* world, idealism identifies the spiritual world with the world of ideas itself. As a result, it is compelled to remain fixed with its world-outlook in the circle of activity of the Ego, as if bewitched.

A curious variant of idealism is to be found in the view which Friedrich Albert Lange has put forward in his widely read *History of Materialism*. He holds that the materialists are quite right in declaring all phenomena, including our thinking, to be the product of purely material processes, but, conversely, matter and its processes are for him themselves the product of our thinking.

> The senses give us only the *effects* of things, not true copies, much less the things themselves. But among these mere effects we must include the senses themselves together with the brain and the molecular vibrations which we assume to go on there.

That is, our thinking is produced by the material processes, and these by the thinking of our I. Lange's philosophy is thus nothing more than the story, in philosophical terms, of the intrepid Baron Münchhausen, who holds himself up in the air by his own pigtail.

The third form of monism is the one which finds even in the simplest entity (the atom) both matter and spirit already united. But nothing is gained by this either, except that the question, which really originates in our consciousness, is shifted to another place. How comes it that the simple entity manifests itself in a two-fold manner, if it is an indivisible unity?

Against all these theories we must urge the fact that we meet with the basic and primary opposition first in our own consciousness. It is we ourselves who break away from the bosom of Nature and contrast ourselves as "I" with the "World". Goethe has given classic expression to this in his essay *Nature*, although his manner may at first sight be considered quite unscientific: "Living in the midst of her (Nature) we are strangers to her. Ceaselessly she speaks to us, yet betrays none of her secrets." But Goethe knows the reverse side too: "Men are all in her and she in all."

However true it may be that we have estranged ourselves from Nature, it is none the less true that we feel we are in her and belong to her. It can be only her own working which pulsates also in us.

We must find the way back to her again. A simple reflection can point this way out to us. We have, it is true, torn ourselves away from Nature, but we must none the less have taken something of her with us into our own being. This element of Nature in us we must seek out, and then we shall find the connection with her once more. Dualism fails to do this. It considers human inwardness as a spiritual entity utterly alien to Nature, and then attempts somehow to hitch it on to Nature. No wonder that it cannot find the connecting link. We can find Nature outside us only if we have first learned to know her *within* us. What is akin to her within us must be our guide. This marks out our path of enquiry. We shall attempt no speculations concerning the interaction of Nature and spirit. Rather shall we probe into the depths of our own being, to find there those elements which we saved in our flight from Nature.

Investigation of our own being must give us the answer to the riddle. We must reach a point where we can say to ourselves, "Here we are no longer merely 'I', here is something which is more than 'I'."

I am well aware that many who have read thus far will not find my discussion "scientific", as this term is used today.

To this I can only reply that I have so far been concerned not with scientific results of any kind, but with the simple description of what every one of us experiences in his own consciousness. The inclusion of a few phrases about attempts to reconcile man's consciousness and the world serves solely to elucidate the actual facts. I have therefore made no attempt to use the various expressions "I", "Spirit", "World", "Nature", in the precise way that is usual in psychology and philosophy. The ordinary consciousness is unaware of the sharp distinctions made by the sciences, and my purpose so far has been solely to record the facts of everyday experience. I am concerned, not with the way in which science, so far, has interpreted consciousness, but with the way in which we experience it in every moment of our lives.

CHAPTER THREE

Thinking in the service of Knowledge

WHEN I observe how a billiard ball, when struck, communicates its motion to another, I remain entirely without influence on the course of this observed process. The direction of motion and the velocity of the second ball are determined by the direction and velocity of the first. As long as I remain a mere spectator, I can only say anything about the movement of the second ball when it has taken place. It is quite different when I begin to reflect on the content of my observation. The purpose of my reflection is to form concepts of the occurrence. I connect the concept of an elastic ball with certain other concepts of mechanics, and take into consideration the special circumstances which obtain in the instance in question. I try, in other words, to add to the occurrence which takes place without my assistance a second process which takes place in the conceptual sphere. This latter one is dependent on me. This is shown by the fact that I can rest content with the observation, and renounce all search for concepts if I have no need of them. If however, this need is present, then I am not satisfied until I have brought the concepts Ball, Elasticity, Motion, Impact, Velocity, etc., into a certain connection, to which the observed process is related in a definite way. As surely as the occurrence goes on independently of me, so surely is the conceptual process unable to take place without my assistance.

We shall have to consider later whether this activity of mine really proceeds from my own independent being, or whether those modern physiologists are right who say that we cannot think as we will, but that we must think just as those thoughts and thought-connections determine that happen to be present in our consciousness.* For the present we wish merely to establish the fact that we constantly feel obliged to seek for concepts and connections of concepts, which stand in a certain relation to the objects and events which are given independently of us. Whether this activity is really *ours* or whether we perform it according to an unalterable necessity, is a question we need not decide at present. That it appears in the first instance to be ours is beyond question. We know for certain that we are not given the concepts together with the objects. That I am myself the agent in the conceptual process may be an illusion, but to immediate observation it certainly appears to be so. The question is, therefore: What do we gain by supplementing an event with a conceptual counterpart?

There is a profound difference between the ways in which, for me, the parts of an event are related to one another before, and after, the discovery of the corresponding concepts. Mere observation can trace the parts of a given event as they occur, but their connection remains obscure without the help of concepts. I see the first billiard ball move towards the second in a certain direction and with a certain velocity. What will happen after the impact I must await, and again I can only follow it with my eyes. Suppose someone, at the moment of impact, obstructs my view of the field where the event is taking place, then, as mere spectator, I remain ignorant of what happens afterwards. The situation is different if prior to the obstruction of my view I have discovered the concepts corresponding to the pattern of

* E.g., Ziehen, *Leitfaden der physiologischen Psychologie*, Jena 1893, p 171.

events. In that case I can say what will happen even when I am no longer able to observe. An event or an object which is merely observed, does not of itself reveal anything about its connection with other events or objects. This connection becomes evident only when observation is combined with thinking.

Observation and *thinking* are the two points of departure for all the spiritual striving of man, in so far as he is conscious of such striving. The workings of common sense, as well as the most complicated scientific researches, rest on these two fundamental pillars of our spirit. Philosophers have started from various primary antitheses: idea and reality, subject and object, appearance and thing-in-itself, "I" and "Not-I", idea and will, concept and matter, force and substance, the conscious and the unconscious. It is easy to show, however, that all these antitheses must be preceded by that of *observation* and *thinking*, this being for man the most important one.

Whatever principle we choose to lay down, we must either prove that somewhere we have observed it, or we must enunciate it in the form of a clear thought which can be re-thought by any other thinker. Every philosopher who sets out to discuss his fundamental principles must express them in conceptual form and thus use thinking. He therefore indirectly admits that his activity presupposes thinking. Whether thinking or something else is the chief factor in the evolution of the world will not be decided at this point. But that *without* thinking, the philosopher can gain no knowledge of such evolution, is clear from the start. In the *occurrence* of the world phenomena, thinking may play a minor part; but in the forming of a *view* about them, there can be no doubt that its part is a leading one.

As regards observation, our need of it is due to the way

we are constituted. Our thinking about a horse and the object "horse" are two things which for us emerge apart from each other. This object is accessible to us only by means of observation. As little as we can form a concept of a horse by merely staring at the animal, just as little are we able by mere thinking to produce a corresponding object.

In sequence of time, observation does in fact come before thinking. For even thinking we must get to know first through observation. It was essentially a description of an observation when, at the beginning of this chapter, we gave an account of how thinking lights up in the presence of an event and goes beyond what is merely presented. Everything that enters the circle of our experience, we first become aware of through observation. The content of sensation, perception and contemplation, all feelings, acts of will, dreams and fancies, mental pictures, concepts and ideas, all illusions and hallucinations, are given to us through *observation*.

But thinking as an *object of observation* differs essentially from all other objects. The observation of a table, or a tree, occurs in me as soon as these objects appear upon the horizon of my experience. Yet I do not, at the same time, observe my thinking about these things. I observe the table, and I carry out the thinking about the table, but I do not at the same moment observe this. I must first take up a standpoint outside my own activity if, in addition to observing the table, I want also to observe my thinking about the table. Whereas observation of things and events, and thinking about them, are everyday occurrences filling up the continuous current of my life, observation of the thinking itself is a kind of exceptional state. This fact must be properly taken into account when we come to determine the relationship of thinking to all other contents of observation. We must be quite clear about the fact that, in observing thinking, we are applying to it a procedure which constitutes the normal course of events for the study of the whole of the rest of the world-content, but which in this normal course of events is not applied to thinking itself.

Someone might object that what I have said about thinking applies equally to feeling and to all other spiritual activities. Thus for instance, when I have a feeling of pleasure, the feeling is also kindled by the object, and it is this object that I observe, but not the feeling of pleasure. This objection, however, is based on an error. Pleasure does not stand at all in the same relation to its object as the concept formed by thinking. I am conscious, in the most positive way, that the concept of a thing is formed through my activity; whereas pleasure is produced in me by an object in the same way as, for instance, a change is caused in an object by a stone which falls on it. For observation, a pleasure is given in exactly the same way as the event which causes it. The same is not true of the concept. I can ask why a particular event arouses in me a feeling of pleasure, but I certainly cannot ask why an event produces in me a particular set of concepts. The question would be simply meaningless. In reflecting upon an event, I am in no way concerned with an effect upon myself. I can learn nothing about myself through knowing the concepts which correspond to the observed change in a pane of glass by a stone thrown against it. But I do very definitely learn something about my personality when I know the feeling which a certain event arouses in me. When I say of an observed object, "This is a rose," I say absolutely nothing about myself; but when I say of the same thing that "it gives me a feeling of pleasure," I characterize not only the rose, but also myself in my relation to the rose.

There can, therefore, be no question of putting thinking and feeling on a level as objects of observation. And the same

25

could easily be shown of other activities of the human spirit. Unlike thinking, they must be classed with other observed objects or events. The peculiar nature of thinking lies just in this, that it is an activity which is directed solely upon the observed object and not on the thinking personality. This is apparent even from the way in which we express our thoughts about an object, as distinct from our feelings or acts of will. When I see an object and recognize it as a table, I do not as a rule say, "I am thinking of a table," but, "this is a table." On the other hand, I do say, "I am pleased with the table." In the former case, I am not at all interested in stating that I have entered into a relation with the table; whereas in the latter case, it is just this relation that matters. In saying, "I am thinking of a table," I already enter the exceptional state characterized above, in which something that is always contained—though not as an observed object—within our spiritual activity, is itself made into an object of observation.

This is just the peculiar nature of thinking, that the thinker forgets his thinking while actually engaged in it. What occupies his attention is not his thinking, but the object of his thinking, which he is observing.

The first observation which we make about thinking is therefore this: that it is the unobserved element in our ordinary mental and spiritual life.

The reason why we do not observe the thinking that goes on in our ordinary life is none other than this, that it is due to our own activity. Whatever I do not myself produce, appears in my field of observation as an object; I find myself confronted by it as something that has come about independently of me. It comes to meet me. I must accept it as something that precedes my thinking process, as a premiss. While I am reflecting upon the object, I am occupied with it, my attention is focussed upon it. To be thus occupied is precisely to *contemplate by thinking.* I attend, not to my activity, but to the object of this activity. In other words, while I am thinking I pay no heed to my thinking, which is of my own making, but only to the *object* of my thinking, which is not of my making.

I am, moreover, in the same position when I enter into the exceptional state and reflect on my own thinking. I can never observe my present thinking; I can only subsequently take my experiences of my thinking process as the object of fresh thinking. If I wanted to watch my present thinking, I should have to split myself into two persons, one to think, the other to observe this thinking. But this I cannot do. I can only accomplish it in two separate acts. The thinking to be observed is never that in which I am actually engaged, but another one. Whether, for this purpose, I make observations of my own former thinking, or follow the thinking process of another person, or finally, as in the example of the motions of the billiard balls, assume an imaginary thinking process, is immaterial.

There are two things which are incompatible with one another: productive activity and the simultaneous contemplation of it. This is recognized even in Genesis (I, 31). Here God creates the world in the first six days, and only when it is there is any contemplation of it possible: "And God saw everything that he had made and, behold, it was very good." The same applies to our thinking. It must be there first, if we would observe it.

The reason why it is impossible to observe thinking in the actual moment of its occurrence, is the very one which makes it possible for us to know it more immediately and more intimately than any other process in the world. Just because it is our own creation do we know the characteristic features of its course, the manner in which the process takes place.

What in all other spheres of observation can be found only indirectly, namely, the relevant context and the relationship between the individual objects, is, in the case of thinking, known to us in an absolutely direct way. I do not on the face of it know why, for my observation, thunder follows lightning; but I know directly, from the very content of the two concepts, why my thinking connects the *concept* of thunder with the *concept* of lightning. It does not matter in the least whether I have the right concepts of lightning and thunder. The connection between those concepts that I do have is clear to me, and this through the very concepts themselves.

This transparent clearness concerning our thinking process is quite independent of our knowledge of the physiological basis of thinking. Here I am speaking of thinking in so far as we know it from the observation of our own spiritual activity. How one material process in my brain causes or influences another while I am carrying out a thinking operation, is quite irrelevant. What I observe about thinking is not what process in my brain connects the concept lightning with the concept thunder but what causes me to bring the two concepts into a particular relationship. My observation shows me that in linking one thought with another there is nothing to guide me but the *content* of my thoughts; I am not guided by any material processes in my brain. In a less materialistic age than our own, this remark would of course be entirely superfluous. Today, however, when there are people who believe that once we know what matter is we shall also know how it thinks, we do have to insist that one may talk about thinking without trespassing on the domain of brain physiology.

Many people today find it difficult to grasp the concept of thinking in its purity. Anyone who challenges the description of thinking which I have given here by quoting Cabanis' statement that "the brain secretes thoughts as the liver does gall or the spittle-glands spittle . . .", simply does not know what I am talking about. He tries to find thinking by a process of mere observation in the same way that we proceed in the case of other objects that make up the world. But he cannot find it in this way because, as I have shown, it eludes just this ordinary observation. Whoever cannot transcend materialism lacks the ability to bring about the exceptional condition I have described, in which he becomes conscious of what in all other spiritual activity remains unconscious. If someone is not willing to take this standpoint, then one can no more discuss thinking with him than one can discuss colour with a blind man. But in any case he must not imagine that we regard physiological processes as thinking. He fails to explain thinking because he simply does not see it.

For everyone, however, who has the ability to observe thinking—and with good will every normal man has this ability—this observation is the most important one he can possibly make. For he observes something of which he himself is the creator; he finds himself confronted, not by an apparently foreign object, but by his own activity. He knows how the thing he is observing comes into being. He sees into its connections and relationships. A firm point has now been reached from which one can, with some hope of success, seek an explanation of all other phenomena of the world.

The feeling that he had found such a firm point led the father of modern philosophy, Descartes, to base the whole of human knowledge on the principle: *I think, therefore I am.* All other things, all other events, are there independently of me. Whether they be truth, or illusion, or dream, I know not. There is only one thing of which I am absolutely certain, for I myself give it its certain existence; and that is my thinking. Whatever other origin it may ultimately have, may it come from God or from elsewhere, of one thing I am certain: that it exists in the sense that I myself bring it forth. Descartes had, to begin with, no justification for giving his statement more meaning than this. All that he had any right to assert was that within the whole world content I apprehend myself in my thinking as in that activity which is most uniquely my own. What the attached *"therefore I am"* is supposed to mean has been much debated. It can have a meaning on one condition only. The simplest assertion I can make of a thing is that it *is*, that it exists. How this existence can be further defined in the case of any particular thing that appears on the horizon of my experience, is at first sight impossible to say. Each object must first be studied in its relation to others before we can determine in what sense it can be said to exist. An experienced event may be a set of percepts or it may be a dream, an hallucination, or something else. In short, I am unable to say in what sense it exists. I cannot gather this from the event in itself, but I shall find it out when I consider the event in its relation to other things. But here again I cannot know *more* than just how it stands in relation to these other things. My investigation touches firm ground only when I find an object which exists in a sense which I can derive from the object itself. But I am myself such an object in that I think, for I give to my existence the definite, self-determined content of the thinking activity. From here I can go on to ask whether other things exist in the same or in some other sense.

When we make thinking an object of observation, we add to the other observed contents of the world something which usually escapes our attention. But the way we stand in relation to the other things is in no way altered. We add to the number of objects of observation, but not to the number of methods. While we are observing the other things, there enters among the processes of the world—among which I now include observation—one process which is overlooked. Something is present which is different from all other processes, something which is not taken into account. But when I observe my own thinking, no such neglected element is present. For what now hovers in the background is once more just thinking itself. The object of observation is qualitatively identical with the activity directed upon it. This is another characteristic feature of thinking. When we make it an object of observation, we are not compelled to do so with the help of something qualitatively different, but can remain within the same element.

When I weave an independently given object into my thinking, I transcend my observation, and the question arises: What right have I to do this? Why do I not simply let the object impress itself upon me? How is it possible for my thinking to be related to the object? These are questions which everyone must put to himself who reflects on his own thought processes. But all these questions cease to exist when we think about thinking itself. We then add nothing to our thinking that is foreign to it, and therefore have no need to justify any such addition.

Schelling says, "To know Nature means to create Nature." If we take these words of this bold Nature-philosopher literally, we shall have to renounce for ever all hope of gaining knowledge of Nature. For Nature is there already, and in order to create it a second time, we must first know the principles according to which it has originated. From the Nature that already exists we should have to borrow or crib the fundamental principles for the Nature we want to *begin* by creating. This borrowing, which would have to precede the creating, would however mean *knowing* Nature, and this would still be so even if after the borrowing no creation were to take place. The only kind of Nature we could create without *first* having knowledge of it would be a Nature that does not yet exist.

What is impossible for us with regard to Nature, namely, creating before knowing, we achieve in the case of thinking. Were we to refrain from thinking until we had first gained knowledge of it, we would never come to it at all. We must resolutely plunge right into the activity of thinking, so that afterwards, by observing what we have done, we may gain knowledge of it. For the observation of *thinking*, we ourselves first create an object; the presence of all *other* objects is taken care of without any activity on our part.

My contention that we must think before we can examine thinking might easily be countered by the apparently equally valid contention that we cannot wait with digesting until we have first observed the process of digestion. This objection would be similar to that brought by Pascal against Descartes, when he asserted that we might also say, "I walk, therefore I am." Certainly I must go straight ahead with digesting and not wait until I have studied the physiological process of digestion. But I could only compare this with the study of thinking if, after digestion, I set myself not to study it by thinking, but to eat and digest it. It is after all not without reason that, whereas digestion cannot become the object of digestion, thinking can very well become the object of thinking.

This then is indisputable, that in thinking we have got hold of one corner of the whole world process which requires our presence if anything is to happen. And this is just the point upon which everything turns. The very reason why things confront me in such a puzzling way is just that I play no part in their production. They are simply given to me, whereas in the case of thinking I know how it is done.

Hence for the study of all that happens in the world there can be no more fundamental starting point than thinking itself.

I should now like to mention a widely current error which prevails with regard to thinking. It is often said that thinking, as it is in itself, is nowhere given to us: the thinking that connects our observations and weaves a network of concepts about them is not at all the same as that which we subsequently extract from the objects of observation in order to make it the object of our study. What we first weave unconsciously into the things is said to be quite different from what we consciously extract from them again.

Those who hold this view do not see that it is impossible in this way to escape from thinking. I cannot get outside thinking when I want to study it. If we want to distinguish between thinking *before* we have become conscious of it, and thinking of which we have *subsequently* become aware, we should not forget that this distinction is a purely external one which has nothing to do with the thing itself. I do not in any way alter a thing by thinking about it. I can well imagine that a being with quite differently constructed sense organs and with a differently functioning intelligence, would have a very different mental picture of a horse from mine, but I cannot imagine that my own thinking becomes something different through the fact that I observe it. I myself observe what I myself produce. Here we are not talking of how my thinking looks to an intelligence other than mine, but of how it looks to me. In any case the picture of *my* thinking which another intelligence might have cannot be a truer one than my own. Only if I were not myself the being doing the thinking, but if the thinking were to confront me as the activity of a being quite foreign to me, might I then say that although my own picture of the thinking may arise in a

33

particular way, what the thinking of that being may be like in itself, I am quite unable to know.

So far, there is not the slightest reason why I should regard my own thinking from any point of view other than my own. After all, I contemplate the rest of the world by means of thinking. Why should I make my thinking an exception?

I believe I have give sufficient reasons for making thinking the starting point for my study of the world. When Archimedes had discovered the lever, he thought he could lift the whole cosmos from its hinges, if only he could find a point of support for his instrument. He needed something that was supported by itself and by nothing else. In thinking we have a principle which subsists through itself. Let us try, therefore, to understand the world starting from this basis. We can grasp thinking by means of itself. The question is, whether we can also grasp anything else through it.

I have so far spoken of thinking without taking account of its vehicle, human consciousness. Most present-day philosophers would object that before there can be thinking, there must be consciousness. Hence we ought to start, not from thinking, but from consciousness. There is no thinking, they say, without consciousness. To this I must reply that in order to clear up the relation between thinking and consciousness, I must think about it. Hence I presuppose thinking. Nevertheless one could still argue that although, when the philosopher tries to understand consciousness he makes use of thinking and to that extent presupposes it, yet in the ordinary course of life thinking does arise within consciousness and therefore presupposes consciousness.

Now if this answer were given to the world creator when he was about to create thinking, it would doubtless be to the point. Naturally it is not possible to create thinking before

34

consciousness. The philosopher, however, is not concerned with creating the world but with understanding it. Accordingly he has to seek the starting points not for the creation of the world but for the understanding of it. It seems to me very strange that the philosopher should be reproached for troubling himself first and foremost about the correctness of his principles instead of turning straight to the objects which he seeks to understand. The world creator had above all to know how to find a vehicle for thinking, but the philosopher has to seek a secure foundation for his attempts to understand what already exists. How does it help us to start with consciousness and subject it to the scrutiny of thinking, if we do not first know whether thinking is in fact able to give us insight into things at all?

We must first consider thinking quite impartially, without reference to a thinking subject or a thought object. For both subject and object are concepts formed by thinking. There is no denying that *before anything else can be understood, thinking must be understood.* Whoever denies this fails to realize that man is not the first link in the chain of creation but the last. Hence, in order to explain the world by means of concepts, we cannot start from the elements of existence which came first in time, but we must begin with that element which is given to us as the nearest and most intimate. We cannot at one bound transport ourselves back to the beginning of the world in order to begin our studies from there, but we must start from the present moment and see whether we can ascend from the later to the earlier. As long as Geology invented fabulous catastrophes to account for the present state of the earth, it groped in darkness. It was only when it began to study the processes at present at work on the earth, and from these to argue back to the past, that it gained a firm foundation. As long as Philosophy goes on assuming all sorts of basic principles, such as atom, motion, matter, will, or the unconscious, it will hang in the air. Only if the philosopher recognizes that which is last in time as his first point of attack, can he reach his goal. This absolutely last thing at which world evolution has arrived is in fact *thinking*.

There are people who say it is impossible to ascertain with certainty whether our thinking is right or wrong, and thus our starting point is in any case a doubtful one. It would be just as sensible to doubt whether a tree is in itself right or wrong. Thinking is a fact, and it is meaningless to speak of the truth or falsity of a fact. I can, at most, be in doubt as to whether thinking is correctly applied, just as I can doubt whether a certain tree supplies wood adapted to the making of this or that useful object. To show how far the application of thinking to the world is right or wrong, is precisely the task of this book. I can understand anyone doubting whether, by means of thinking, we can gain knowledge of the world, but it is incomprehensible to me how anyone can doubt the rightness of thinking in itself.

Author's addition, 1918

In the preceding discussion I have pointed out the significant difference between thinking and all other activities of the soul, as a fact which presents itself to genuinely unprejudiced observation. Anyone who does not strive towards this unprejudiced observation will be tempted to bring against my arguments such objections as these: When I think about a rose, this after all only expresses a relation of my "I" to the rose, just as when I feel the beauty of the rose. There is a relation between "I" and object in the case of thinking just as much as in the case of feeling or perceiving. Such an objection leaves out of account the fact that *only* in the thinking activity does the "I" know itself to be *one and the same being with that which is active*, right into all the ramifications of this activity. With no other soul activity is this so completely the case. For example, in a feeling of pleasure it is perfectly possible for a more delicate observation to discriminate between the extent to which the "I" knows itself to be *one and the same being with what is active*, and the extent to which there is something passive in the "I" to which the pleasure merely presents itself. The same applies to the other soul activities. Above all one should not confuse the "having of thought-images" with the elaboration of thought by thinking. Thought-images may appear in the soul after the fashion of dreams, like vague intimations. But this is not *thinking*. True, someone might now say: If this is what you mean by "thinking", then your thinking involves willing and you have to do not merely with thinking but also with the will in the thinking. However, this would simply justify us in saying: Genuine thinking must always be willed.

37

But this is quite irrelevant to the characterization of thinking as this has been given in the preceding discussion. Granted that the nature of thinking necessarily implies its being *willed*, the point that matters is that nothing is willed which, in being carried out, does not appear to the "I" as an activity completely its own and under its own supervision. Indeed, we must say that owing to the very nature of thinking as here defined, it *must* appear to the observer as willed through and through. If we really make the effort to grasp everything that is relevant to a judgment about the nature of thinking, we cannot fail to see that this soul activity does have the unique character we have here described.

A person whom the author of this book rates very highly as a thinker has objected that it is impossible to speak about thinking as we are doing here, because what one believes oneself to have observed as active thinking is nothing but an illusion. In reality one is observing only the results of an unconscious activity which lies at the basis of thinking. Only because this unconscious activity is not observed does the illusion arise that the observed thinking exists in its own right, just as when in an illumination by means of a rapid succession of electric sparks we believe that we are seeing a continuous movement. This objection, too, rests only on an inaccurate view of the facts. In making it, one forgets that it is the "I" itself which, from its standpoint *inside* the thinking, observes its *own* activity. The "I" would have to stand outside the thinking in order to suffer the sort of deception which is caused by an illumination with a rapid succession of electric sparks. It would be much truer to say that precisely in using such an analogy one is forcibly deceiving oneself, just as if someone seeing a moving light were to insist that it is being freshly lit by an unknown hand at every point where it appears. No, whoever is determined to see in thinking anything other than a clearly surveyable activity produced by the "I" itself, must first shut his eyes to the plain facts that are there for the seeing, in order then to invent a hypothetical activity as the basis of thinking. If he does not thus blind himself, he will have to recognize that everything which he "thinks up" in this way as an addition to the thinking only leads him away from its real nature. Unprejudiced observation shows that nothing is to be counted as belonging to the nature of thinking except what is found *in* thinking itself. One will never arrive at something which is the *cause* of thinking if one steps outside the realm of thinking itself.

CHAPTER FOUR

The World as Percept

THROUGH thinking, *concepts* and *ideas* arise. What a concept is cannot be expressed in words. Words can do no more than draw our attention to the fact that we have concepts. When someone sees a tree, his thinking reacts to his observation, an ideal element is added to the object, and he considers the object and the ideal counterpart as belonging together. When the object disappears from his field of observation, only the ideal counterpart of it remains. This latter is the *concept* of the object. The more our range of experience is widened, the greater becomes the sum of our concepts. But concepts certainly do not stand isolated from one another. They combine to form a systematically ordered whole. The concept "organism", for instance, links up with those of "orderly development" and "growth". Other concepts which are based on *single* objects merge together into a unity. All concepts I may form of lions merge into the collective concept "lion". In this way all the separate concepts combine to form a closed conceptual system in which each has its special place. *Ideas* do not differ qualitatively from concepts. They are but fuller, more saturated, more comprehensive concepts. I must attach special importance to the necessity of bearing in mind, here, that I make *thinking* my starting point, and not *concepts* and *ideas* which are first gained by means of thinking. For these latter already presuppose thinking. My remarks regarding the self-supporting and self-determined nature of thinking cannot, therefore, be simply transferred to concepts. (I make special mention of this, because it is here that I differ from Hegel, who regards the concept as something primary and original.)

Concepts cannot be gained through observation. This follows from the simple fact that the growing human being only slowly and gradually forms the concepts corresponding to the objects which surround him. Concepts are *added* to observation.

A philosopher widely read at the present day—Herbert Spencer—describes the mental process which we carry out with respect to observation as follows:

> If, when walking through the fields some day in September, you hear a rustle a few yards in advance, and on observing the ditch-side where it occurs, see the herbage agitated, you will probably turn towards the spot to learn by what this sound and motion are produced. As you approach there flutters into the ditch a partridge; on seeing which your curiosity is satisfied— you have what you call an *explanation* of the appearances. The explanation, mark, amounts to this; that whereas throughout life you have had countless experiences of disturbance among small stationary bodies, accompanying the movement of other bodies among them, and have generalized the relation between such disturbances and such movements, you consider this particular disturbance explained on finding it to present an instance of the like relation.*

A closer analysis shows matters to stand very differently from the way described above. When I hear a noise, I first look for the concept which fits this observation. It is this concept which first leads me beyond the mere noise. If one thinks no further, one simply hears the noise and is content to leave it at that. But my reflecting makes it clear to me that I have to regard the noise as an effect. Therefore not until I have connected the concept of *effect* with the perception of

* *First Principles*, Part I, 23.

the noise, do I feel the need to go beyond the solitary observation and look for the *cause*. The concept of *effect* calls up that of *cause*, and my next step is to look for the object which is being the cause, which I find in the shape of the partridge. But these concepts, cause and effect, I can never gain through mere observation, however many instances the observation may cover. Observation evokes thinking, and it is thinking that first shows me how to link one separate experience to another.

If one demands of a "strictly objective science" that it should take its content from observation alone, then one must at the same time demand that it should forgo all thinking. For thinking, by its very nature, goes beyond what is observed.

We must now pass from thinking to the being that thinks; for it is through the thinker that thinking is combined with observation. Human consciousness is the stage upon which concept and observation meet and become linked to one another. In saying this we have in fact characterized this (human) consciousness. It is the mediator between thinking and observation. In as far as we observe a thing it appears to us as *given*; in as far as we think, we appear to ourselves as being *active*. We regard the thing as *object* and ourselves as thinking *subject*. Because we direct our thinking upon our observation, we have consciousness of objects; because we direct it upon ourselves, we have consciousness of ourselves, or *self-consciousness*. Human consciousness must of necessity be at the same time self-consciousness because it is a consciousness which *thinks*. For when thinking contemplates its own activity, it makes its own essential being, as subject, into a *thing*, as object.

It must, however, not be overlooked that only with the help of thinking am I able to determine myself as subject and contrast myself with objects. Therefore thinking must never be regarded as a merely subjective activity. Thinking lies *beyond* subject and object. It produces these two concepts just as it produces all others. When, therefore, I, as thinking subject, refer a concept to an object, we must not regard this reference as something purely subjective. It is not the subject that makes the reference, but thinking. The subject does not think because it is a subject; rather it appears to itself as subject because it can think. The activity exercised by man as a *thinking* being is thus not merely subjective. Rather is it something neither subjective nor objective, that transcends both these concepts. I ought never to say that my individual subject thinks, but much more that my individual subject lives by the grace of thinking. Thinking is thus an element which leads me out beyond myself and connects me with the objects. But at the same time it separates me from them, inasmuch as it sets me, as subject, over against them.

It is just this which constitutes the double nature of man. He thinks, and thereby embraces both himself and the rest of the world. But at the same time it is by means of thinking that he determines himself as an *individual* confronting the *things*.

We must next ask ourselves how that other element, which we have so far simply called the object of observation and which meets the thinking in our consciousness, comes into our consciousness at all.

In order to answer this question we must eliminate from our field of observation everything that has been imported by thinking. For at any moment the content of our consciousness will already be interwoven with concepts in the most varied ways.

We must imagine that a being with fully developed human

43

intelligence originates out of nothing and confronts the world. What it would be aware of, before it sets its thinking in motion, would be the pure content of observation. The world would then appear to this being as nothing but a mere disconnected aggregate of *objects of sensation*: colours, sounds, sensations of pressure, of warmth, of taste and smell; also feelings of pleasure and pain. This aggregate is the content of pure, unthinking observation. Over against it stands thinking, ready to begin its activity as soon as a point of attack presents itself. Experience shows at once that this does happen. Thinking is able to draw threads from one element of observation to another. It links definite concepts with these elements and thereby establishes a relationship between them. We have already seen how a noise which we hear becomes connected with another observation by our identifying the former as the effect of the latter.

If now we recollect that the activity of thinking is on no account to be considered as merely subjective, then we shall also not be tempted to believe that the relationships thus established by thinking have merely subjective validity.

Our next task is to discover by means of thoughtful reflection what relation the immediately given content of observation mentioned above has to the conscious subject.

The ambiguity of current speech makes it necessary for me to come to an agreement with my readers concerning the use of a word which I shall have to employ in what follows. I shall apply the word "percept" to the immediate objects of sensation enumerated above, in so far as the conscious subject apprehends them through observation. It is, then, not the *process* of observation but the *object* of observation which I call the "percept".

I do not choose the term "sensation", since this has a definite meaning in physiology which is narrower than that

44

of my concept of "percept". I can speak of a feeling in myself (emotion) as percept, but not as sensation in the physiological sense of the term. Even my feeling becomes known to me by becoming a *percept* for me. And the way in which we gain knowledge of our thinking through observation is such that thinking too, in its first appearance for our consciousness, may be called a percept.

The naïve man regards his percepts, such as they appear to his immediate apprehension, as things having an existence wholly independent of him. When he sees a tree he believes in the first instance that it stands in the form which he sees, with the colours of its various parts, and so on, there on the spot towards which his gaze is directed. When the same man sees the sun in the morning appear as a disc on the horizon, and follows the course of this disc, he believes that all this actually exists and happens just as he observes it. To this belief he clings until he meets with further percepts which contradict his former ones. The child who as yet has no experience of distance grasps at the moon, and only corrects its picture of the reality, based on first impressions, when a second percept contradicts the first. Every extension of the circle of my percepts compels me to correct my picture of the world. We see this in everyday life, as well as in the spiritual development of mankind. The picture which the ancients made for themselves of the relation of the earth to the sun and other heavenly bodies had to be replaced by another when Copernicus found that it was not in accordance with some percepts, which in those early days were unknown. A man who had been born blind said, when operated on by Dr Franz, that the picture of the size of objects which he had formed by his sense of touch before his operation, was a very different one. He had to correct his tactual percepts by his visual percepts.

45

How is it that we are compelled to make these continual corrections to our observations?

A simple reflection gives the answer to this question. When I stand at one end of an avenue, the trees at the other end, away from me, seem smaller and nearer together than those where I stand. My percept-picture changes when I change the place from which I am looking. Therefore the form in which it presents itself to me is dependent on a condition which is due not to the object but to me, the perceiver. It is all the same to the avenue wherever I stand. But the picture I have of it depends essentially on just this viewpoint. In the same way, it makes no difference to the sun and the planetary system that human beings happen to look at them from the earth; but the percept-picture of the heavens presented to them is determined by the fact that they inhabit the earth. This dependence of our percept-picture on our place of observation is the easiest one to understand. The matter becomes more difficult when we realize how our world of percepts is dependent on our bodily and spiritual organization. The physicist shows us that within the space in which we hear a sound there are vibrations of the air, and also that the body in which we seek the origin of the sound exhibits a vibrating movement of its parts. We perceive this movement as sound only if we have a normally constructed ear. Without this the world would be for ever silent for us. Physiology tells us that there are people who perceive nothing of the magnificent splendour of colour which surrounds us. Their percept-picture has only degrees of light and dark. Others are blind only to one colour, for example, red. Their world picture lacks this hue, and hence it is actually a different one from that of the average man. I should like to call the dependence of my percept-picture on my place of observation, "mathematical", and its dependence on my organization, "qualitative". The former determines the proportions of size and mutual distances of my percepts, the latter their quality. The fact that I see a red surface as red—this qualitative determination—depends on the organization of my eye.

My percept-pictures, then, are in the first instance subjective. The recognition of the subjective character of our percepts may easily lead us to doubt whether there is any objective basis for them at all. When we realize that a percept, for example that of a red colour or of a certain tone, is not possible without a specific structure of our organism, we may easily be led to believe that it has no permanency apart from our subjective organization and that, were it not for our act of perceiving it as an object, it would not exist in any sense. The classical representative of this view is George Berkeley, who held that from the moment we realize the importance of the *subject* for perception, we are no longer able to believe in the existence of a world without a conscious Spirit.

> Some truths there are so near and obvious to the mind that man need only open his eyes to see them. Such I take this important one to be, to wit, that all the choir of heaven and furniture of the earth, in a word, all those bodies which compose the mighty frame of the world, have not any subsistence without a mind, that their *being is* to be perceived or known; that, consequently, so long as they are not actually perceived by me, or do not exist in my mind or that of any other *created spirit*, they must either have no existence at all, *or else subsist in the mind of some Eternal Spirit.**

On this view, when we take away the fact of its being perceived, nothing remains of the percept. There is no colour when none is seen, no sound when none is heard.

* Berkeley, *Principles of Human Knowledge*, Part I, Section 6.

Extension, form, and motion exist as little as colour and sound apart from the act of perception. Nowhere do we see bare extension or shape, but these are always bound up with colour or some other quality unquestionably dependent upon our subjectivity. If these latter disappear when we cease to perceive them, then the former, being bound up with them, must disappear likewise.

To the objection that there must be things that exist apart from consciousness and to which the conscious percept-pictures are similar, even though figure, colour, sound, and so on, have no existence except within the act of perceiving, the above view would answer that a colour can be similar only to a colour, a figure only to a figure. Our percepts can be similar only to our percepts and to nothing else. Even what we call an object is nothing but a collection of percepts which are connected in a particular way. If I strip a table of its shape, extension, colour, etc.—in short, of all that is merely my percept—then nothing remains over. This view, followed up logically, leads to the assertion that the objects of my perceptions exist only through me, and indeed only in as far as, and as long as, I perceive them; they disappear with my perceiving and have no meaning apart from it. Apart from my percepts, I know of no objects and cannot know of any.

No objection can be made to this assertion as long as I am merely referring to the general fact that the percept is partly determined by the organization of myself as subject. The matter would appear very different if we were in a position to say just what part is played by our perceiving in the bringing forth of a percept. We should then know what happens to a percept while it is being perceived, and we should also be able to determine what character it must already possess before it comes to be perceived.

This leads us to turn our attention from the object of perception to the subject of perception. I perceive not only other things, but also myself. The percept of myself contains, to begin with, the fact that I am the stable element in contrast to the continual coming and going of the percept-pictures. The percept of my "I" can always come up in my consciousness while I am having other percepts. When I am absorbed in the perception of a given object I am for the time being aware only of this object. To this the percept of my self can be added. I am then conscious not only of the object but also of my own personality which confronts the object and observes it. I do not merely see a tree, but I also know that *it is I* who am seeing it. I know, moreover, that something happens in me while I am observing the tree. When the tree disappears from my field of vision, an after-effect of this process remains in my consciousness—a picture of the tree. This picture has become associated with my self during my observation. My self has become enriched; its content has absorbed a new element. This element I call my *mental picture* of the tree. I should never have occasion to speak of *mental pictures* did I not experience them in the percept of my own self. Percepts would come and go; I should let them slip by. Only because I perceive my self, and observe that with each percept the content of my self, too, is changed, am I compelled to connect the observation of the object with the changes in my own condition, and to speak of *my mental picture.*

I perceive the mental picture in my self in the same sense as I perceive colour, sound, etc., in other objects. I am now also able to distinguish these other objects that confront me, by calling them the *outer world*, whereas the content of my percept of my self I call my *inner world*. The failure to recognize the true relationship between mental picture and object has led to the greatest misunderstandings in modern philosophy. The perception of a change in me, the modification my self undergoes, has been thrust into the foreground, while the object which causes this modification is lost sight of altogether. It has been said that we perceive not objects but only our mental pictures. I know, so it is said, nothing of the table in itself, which is the object of my observation, but only of the change which occurs within me while I am perceiving the table. This view should not be confused with the Berkeleyan theory mentioned above. Berkeley maintains the subjective nature of the content of my percepts, but he does not say that my knowledge is limited to my mental pictures. He limits my knowledge to my mental pictures because, in his opinion, there are no objects apart from mental picturing. What I take to be a table no longer exists, according to Berkeley, when I cease to look at it. This is why Berkeley holds that my percepts arise directly through the omnipotence of God. I see a table because God calls up this percept in me. For Berkeley, therefore, there are no real beings other than God and human spirits. What we call the "world" exists only in these spirits. What the naïve man calls the outer world, or corporeal nature, is for Berkeley non-existent. This theory is confronted by the now predominant Kantian view which limits our knowledge of the world to our mental pictures, not because it is convinced that things cannot exist beyond these mental pictures, but because it believes us to be so organized that we can experience only the changes of our own selves, but not the things-in-themselves that cause these changes. This view concludes from the fact that I know only my mental pictures, not that there is no reality independent of them, but only that the subject cannot directly assimilate such reality. The subject can merely, "through the medium of its subjective thoughts, imagine it, invent it, think it, cognize it, or perhaps even fail to cognize it."* This (Kantian) conception believes it gives expression to something absolutely certain, something which is immediately evident, requiring no proof.

The first fundamental proposition which the philosopher must bring to clear consciousness is the recognition that our knowledge, *to begin with*, is limited to our mental pictures. Our mental pictures are the only things that we know directly, experience directly; and just because we have direct experience of them, even the most radical doubt cannot rob us of our knowledge of them. On the other hand, the knowledge which goes beyond my mental pictures—taking mental pictures here in the widest possible sense, so as to include all psychical processes—is not proof against doubt. Hence, *at the very beginning of all philosophizing* we must explicitly set down all knowledge which goes beyond mental pictures as being open to doubt.

These are the opening sentences of Volkelt's book on *Immanuel Kant's Theory of Knowledge*. What is here put forward as an immediate and self-evident truth is in reality the result of a thought operation which runs as follows: The naïve man believes that things, just as we perceive them, exist also outside our consciousness. Physics, physiology, and psychology, however, seem to teach us that for our percepts our organization is necessary, and that therefore we cannot know anything about external objects except what our organization transmits to us. Our percepts are thus modifications of our organization, not things-in-themselves. This train of thought has in fact been characterized by Eduard von Hartmann as the one which must lead to the conviction that we can have direct knowledge only of our mental

* O. Liebmann, *Zur Analysis der Wirklichkeit*, p 28.

pictures.* Because, outside our organism, we find vibrations
of physical bodies and of the air which are perceived by us as
sound, it is concluded that what we call sound is nothing
more than a subjective reaction of our organism to these
motions in the external world. Similarly, it is concluded that
colour and warmth are merely modifications of our organism.
And, further, these two kinds of percepts are held to be
produced in us through processes in the external world
which are utterly different from what we experience as
warmth or as colour. When these processes stimulate
the nerves in my skin, I have the subjective percept of
warmth; when they stimulate the optic nerve, I perceive
light and colour. Light, colour, and warmth, then, are the
responses of my sensory nerves to external stimuli. Even
the sense of touch reveals to me, not the objects of the outer
world, but only states of my own body. In the sense of
modern physics one could somehow think that bodies
consist of infinitely small particles called molecules, and that
these molecules are not in direct contact, but are at certain
distances from one another. Between them, therefore, is
empty space. Across this space they act on one another by
forces of attraction and repulsion. If I put my hand on a
body, the molecules of my hand by no means touch those of
the body directly, but there remains a certain distance between body and hand, and what I experience as the body's resis-
tance is nothing but the effect of the force of repulsion which
its molecules exert on my hand. I am absolutely external
to the body and perceive only its effects on my organism.

In amplification of this discussion, there is the theory of
the so-called Specific Nerve Energies, advanced by J.
Müller (1801–1858). It asserts that each sense has the
peculiarity that it responds to all external stimuli in one

* See his *Das Grundproblem der Erkenntnistheorie*, pp. 16-40.

particular way only. If the optic nerve is stimulated, perception of light results, irrespective of whether the stimulation is due to what we call light, or whether mechanical pressure or an electric current works upon the nerve. On the other hand, the same external stimulus applied to different senses gives rise to different percepts. The conclusion from these facts seems to be that our senses can transmit only what occurs in themselves, but nothing of the external world. They determine our percepts, each according to its own nature.

Physiology shows that there can be no direct knowledge even of the effects which objects produce on our sense organs. Through following up the processes which occur in our own bodies, the physiologist finds that, even in the sense organs, the effects of the external movement are transformed in the most manifold ways. We can see this most clearly in the case of eye and ear. Both are very complicated organs which modify the external stimulus considerably before they conduct it to the corresponding nerve. From the peripheral end of the nerve the already modified stimulus is then conducted to the brain. Only now can the central organs be stimulated. Therefore it is concluded that the external process undergoes a series of transformations before it reaches consciousness. What goes on in the brain is connected by so many intermediate links with the external process, that any similarity to the latter is out of the question. What the brain ultimately transmits to the soul is neither external processes, nor processes in the sense organs, but only such as occur in the brain. But even these are not perceived directly by the soul. What we finally have in consciousness are not brain processes at all, but *sensations*. My sensation of *red* has absolutely no similarity to the process which occurs in the brain when I sense red. The

53

redness, again, only appears as an effect in the soul, and the brain process is merely its cause. This is why Hartmann says, "What the subject perceives, therefore, are always only modifications of his own psychical states and nothing else."* When I have the sensations, however, they are as yet very far from being grouped into what I perceive as "things". Only single sensations can be transmitted to me by the brain. The sensations of hardness and softness are transmitted to me by the sense of touch, those of colour and light by the sense of sight. Yet all these are to be found united in one and the same object. This unification, therefore, can only be brought about by the soul itself; that is, the soul combines the separate sensations, mediated through the brain, into bodies. My brain conveys to me singly, and by widely different paths, the visual, tactile, and auditory sensations which the soul then combines into the mental picture of a trumpet. It is just this very last link in a process (the mental picture of the trumpet) which for my consciousness is the very first thing that is given. In it nothing can any longer be found of what exists outside me and originally made an impression on my senses. The external object has been entirely lost on the way to the brain and through the brain to the soul.

It would be hard to find in the history of human culture another edifice of thought which has been built up with greater ingenuity, and which yet, on closer analysis, collapses into nothing. Let us look a little closer at the way it has been constructed. One starts with what is given in naïve consciousness, with the thing as perceived. Then one shows that none of the qualities which we find in this thing would exist for us had we no sense organs. No eye—no colour. Therefore the colour is not yet present in that which affects

* *Das Grundproblem der Erkenntnistheorie*, p. 37.

54

the eye. It arises first through the interaction of the eye and the object. The latter is, therefore, colourless. But neither is the colour in the eye, for in the eye there is only a chemical or physical process which is first conducted by the optic nerve to the brain, and there initiates another process. Even this is not yet the colour. That is only produced in the soul by means of the brain process. Even then it does not yet enter my consciousness, but is first transferred by the soul to a body in the external world. There, upon this body, I finally believe myself to perceive it. We have travelled in a complete circle. We became conscious of a coloured body. That is the first thing. Here the thought operation starts. If I had no eye, the body would be, for me, colourless. I cannot therefore attribute the colour to the body. I start on the search for it. I look for it in the eye—in vain; in the nerve—in vain; in the brain—in vain once more; in the soul—here I find it indeed, but not attached to the body. I find the coloured body again only on returning to my starting point. The circle is completed. I believe that I am cognizing as a product of my soul that which the naïve man regards as existing outside him, in space.

As long as one stops here everything seems to fit beautifully. But we must go over the whole thing again from the beginning. Hitherto I have been dealing with something— the external percept—of which, from my naïve standpoint, I have had until now a totally wrong conception. I thought that the percept, just as I perceive it, had objective existence. But now I observe that it disappears together with my mental picture, that it is only a modification of my inner state of soul. Have I, then, any right at all to start from it in my arguments? Can I say of it that it acts on my soul? I must henceforth treat the table, of which formerly I believed that it acted on me and produced a mental picture of itself in me, as itself a mental picture. But from this it follows logically that my sense organs and the processes in them are also merely subjective. I have no right to speak of a real eye but only of my mental picture of the eye. Exactly the same is true of the nerve paths, and the brain process, and no less of the process in the soul itself, through which things are supposed to be built up out of the chaos of manifold sensations. If, assuming the truth of the first circle of argumentation, I run through the steps of my act of cognition once more, the latter reveals itself as a tissue of mental pictures which, as such, cannot act on one another. I cannot say that my mental picture of the object acts on my mental picture of the eye, and that from this interaction my mental picture of colour results. Nor is it necessary that I should say this. For as soon as I see clearly that my sense organs and their activity, my nerve and soul processes, can also be known to me only through perception, the train of thought which I have outlined reveals itself in its full absurdity. It is quite true that I can have no percept without the corresponding sense organ. But just as little can I be aware of a sense organ without perception. From the percept of a table I can pass to the eye which sees it, or the nerves in the skin which touch it, but what takes place in these I can, in turn, learn only from perception. And then I soon notice that there is no trace of similarity between the process which takes place in the eye and the colour which I perceive. I cannot eliminate my colour percept by pointing to the process which takes place in the eye during this perception. No more can I rediscover the colour in the nerve or brain processes. I only add new percepts, localized within the organism, to the first percept, which the naïve man localizes outside his organism. I merely pass from one percept to another.

Moreover there is a gap in the whole argument. I can

follow the processes in my organism up to those in my brain, even though my assumptions become more and more hypothetical as I approach the central processes of the brain. The path of *external* observation ceases with the process in my brain, more particularly with the process which I should observe if I could deal with the brain using the instruments and methods of physics and chemistry. The path of *inner* observation begins with the sensation, and continues up to the building of *things* out of the material of sensation. At the point of transition from brain process to sensation, the path of observation is interrupted.

The way of thinking here described, known as critical idealism, in contrast to the standpoint of naïve consciousness known as naïve realism, makes the mistake of characterizing the *one* percept as mental picture while taking the other in the very same sense as does the naïve realism which it apparently refutes. It wants to prove that percepts have the character of mental pictures by naïvely accepting the percepts connected with one's own organism as objectively valid facts; and over and above this, it fails to see that it confuses two spheres of observation, between which it can find no connection.

Critical idealism can refute naïve realism only by itself assuming, in naïve-realistic fashion, that one's own organism has objective existence. As soon as the idealist realizes that the percepts connected with his own organism are exactly of the same nature as those which naïve realism assumes to have objective existence, he can no longer use those percepts as a safe foundation for his theory. He would have to regard even his own subjective organization as a mere complex of mental pictures. But this removes the possibility of regarding the content of the perceived world as a product of our spiritual organization. One would have to assume that the mental picture "colour" was only a modification of the mental picture "eye". So-called critical idealism cannot be *proved* without borrowing from naïve realism. Naïve realism can be *refuted* only if, in another sphere, its own assumptions are accepted without proof as being valid.

This much, then, is certain: Investigation within the world of percepts cannot establish critical idealism, and consequently, cannot strip percepts of their objective character.

Still less can the principle *"the perceived world is my mental picture"* be claimed as obvious and needing no proof. Schopenhauer begins his chief work* with the words:

> The world is my mental picture—this is a truth which holds good for everything that lives and cognizes, though man alone can bring it into reflective and abstract consciousness. If he really does this, he has attained to philosophical discretion. It then becomes clear and certain to him that he knows no sun and no earth, but only an eye that sees a sun, a hand that feels an earth; that the world which surrounds him is there only as mental picture, that is, only in relation to something else, to the one who pictures it, which is he himself. If any truth can be asserted *a priori*, it is this one, for it is the expression of that form of all possible and thinkable experience which is more universal than all others, than time, space, or causality, for all these presuppose it . . .

This whole theory is wrecked by the fact, already mentioned, that the eye and the hand are percepts no less than the sun and the earth. Using Schopenhauer's expressions in his own sense, we could reply: My eye that sees the sun, my hand that feels the earth, are my mental pictures just as much as the sun and the earth themselves. That with this the whole theory cancels itself, is clear without further argu-

* *Die Welt als Wille und Vorstellung.*

ment. For only my real eye and my real hand could have the mental pictures "sun" and "earth" as modifications of themselves; the mental pictures "eye" and "hand" cannot have them. Yet it is only of these mental pictures that critical idealism is allowed to speak.

Critical idealism is totally unfitted to form an opinion about the relationship between percept and mental picture. It cannot begin to make the distinction, mentioned on page 48, between what happens to the percept in the process of perception and what must be inherent in it prior to perception. We must, therefore, tackle this problem in another way.

CHAPTER FIVE

The Act of Knowing

FROM the foregoing considerations it follows that it is impossible to prove by investigating the content of our observation that our percepts are mental pictures. Such proof is supposed to be established by showing that, if the process of perceiving takes place in the way in which—on the basis of naïve-realistic assumptions about our psychological and physiological constitution—we imagine that it does, then we have to do, not with things in themselves, but only with our mental pictures of things. Now if naïve realism, when consistently thought out, leads to results which directly contradict its presuppositions, then these presuppositions must be discarded as unsuitable for the foundation of a universal philosophy. In any case, it is not permissible to reject the presuppositions and yet accept the consequences, as the critical idealist does when he bases his assertion that the world is my mental picture on the line of argument already described. (Eduard von Hartmann gives a full account of this line of argument in his work *Das Grundproblem der Erkenntnistheorie*.)

The truth of critical idealism is one thing, the force of its proof another. How it stands with the former will appear later on in the course of this book, but the force of its proof is exactly nil. If one builds a house, and the ground floor collapses while the first floor is being built, then the first floor collapses too. Naïve realism and critical idealism are related as the ground floor to the first floor in this simile.

For someone who believes that the whole perceived world

is only an imagined one, a mental picture, and is in fact the effect upon my soul of things unknown to me, the real problem of knowledge is naturally concerned not with the mental pictures present only in the soul but with the things which are independent of us and which lie outside our consciousness. He asks: How much can we learn about these things *indirectly*, seeing that we cannot observe them *directly*? From this point of view, he is concerned not with the inner connection of his conscious percepts with one another but with their causes which transcend his consciousness and exist independently of him, since the percepts, in his opinion, disappear as soon as he turns his senses away from the things. Our consciousness, on this view, works like a mirror from which the pictures of definite things disappear the moment its reflecting surface is not turned towards them. If, now, we do not see the things themselves but only their reflections, then we must learn indirectly about the nature of the things by drawing conclusions from the behaviour of the reflections. Modern science takes this attitude in that it uses percepts only as a last resort in obtaining information about the processes of matter which lie behind them, and which alone really "are". If the philosopher, as critical idealist, admits real existence at all, then his search for knowledge through the medium of mental pictures is directed solely towards this existence. His interest skips over the subjective world of mental pictures and goes straight for what produces these pictures.

The critical idealist can, however, go even further and say: I am confined to the world of my mental pictures and cannot escape from it. If I think of a thing as being behind my mental picture, this thought is again nothing but a mental picture. An idealist of this type will either deny the thing-in-itself entirely or at any rate assert that it has no significance for human beings, in other words, that it is as good as non-existent since we can know nothing of it.

To this kind of critical idealist the whole world seems a dream, in the face of which all striving for knowledge would be simply meaningless. For him there can be only two sorts of men: victims of the illusion that their own dream structures are real things, and wise men who see through the nothingness of this dream world and who must therefore gradually lose all desire to trouble themselves further about it. From this point of view, even one's own personality may become a mere dream phantom. Just as during sleep there appears among my dream images an image of myself, so in waking consciousness the mental picture of my own I is added to the mental picture of the outer world. We have then given to us in consciousness, not our real I, but only our mental picture of our I. Whoever denies that things exist, or at least that we can know anything of them, must also deny the existence, or at least the knowledge, of one's own personality. The critical idealist then comes to the conclusion that "All reality resolves itself into a wonderful dream, without a life which the dream is about, and without a spirit which is having the dream; into a dream which hangs together in a dream of itself."*

For the person who believes that he recognizes our immediate life to be a dream, it is immaterial whether he postulates nothing more behind this dream or whether he relates his mental pictures to actual things. In both cases life must lose all academic interest for him. But whereas all learning must be meaningless for those who believe that the whole of the accessible universe is exhausted in dreams, yet for others who feel entitled to argue from mental pictures to *things*, learning will consist in the investigation of these "things-in-

* See Fichte, *Die Bestimmung des Menschen.*

themselves." The first of these theories may be called absolute *illusionism*, the second is called *transcendental realism* by its most rigorously logical exponent, Eduard von Hartmann.*

Both these points of view have this in common with naïve realism, that they seek to gain a footing in the world by means of an investigation of percepts. Within this sphere, however, they are unable to find any firm foundation.

One of the most important questions for an adherent of transcendental realism would have to be: How does the Ego produce the world of mental pictures out of itself? A world of mental pictures which was given to us, and which disappeared as soon as we shut our senses to the external world, might kindle an earnest desire for knowledge, in so far as it was a means for investigating indirectly the world of the I-in-itself. If the things of our experience were "mental pictures" then our everyday life would be like a dream, and the discovery of the true state of affairs like waking. Now our dream images interest us as long as we dream and consequently do not detect their dream character. But as soon as we wake, we no longer look for the inner connections of our dream images among themselves, but rather for the physical, physiological, and psychological processes which underlie them. In the same way, a philosopher who holds the world to be his mental picture cannot be interested in the mutual

* Knowledge is called *transcendental* in the sense of this theory when it believes itself to be conscious that nothing can be asserted directly about the thing-in-itself, but makes indirect inferences from the subjective, which is known, to the unknown which lies beyond the subjective (transcendental). The thing-in-itself is, according to this view, beyond the sphere of the *directly* knowable world; in other words, it is transcendent. Our world can, however, be transcendentally related to the transcendent. Hartmann's theory is called realism because it proceeds from the subjective, the ideal, to the transcendent, the real.

relations of the details within this picture. If he allows the existence of a real Ego at all, then his question will be, not how one of his mental pictures is linked with another, but what takes place in the independently existing soul while a certain train of mental pictures passes through his consciousness. If I dream that I am drinking wine which makes my throat burn, and then wake up with a cough,* I cease, the moment I wake, to be interested in the progress of the dream for its own sake. My attention is now concerned only with the physiological and psychological processes by means of which the irritation which causes me to cough comes to be symbolically expressed in the dream picture. Similarly, once the philosopher is convinced that the given world consists of nothing but mental pictures, his interest is bound to switch at once from this world to the real soul which lies behind. The matter is more serious, however, for the adherent of illusionism who denies altogether the existence of an Ego-in-itself behind the mental pictures, or at least holds this Ego to be unknowable. We might very easily be led to such a view by the observation that, in contrast to dreaming, there is indeed the waking state in which we have the opportunity of seeing through our dreams and referring them to the real relations of things, but that there is no state of the self which is related similarly to our waking conscious life. Whoever takes this view fails to see that there is, in fact, something which is related to mere perceiving in the way that our waking experience is related to our dreaming. *This something is thinking.*

The naïve man cannot be charged with the lack of insight referred to here. He accepts life as it is, and regards things as real just as they present themselves to him in experience. The first step, however, which we take beyond this stand-

* See Weygandt, *Entstehung der Träume*, 1893.

64

point can be only this, that we ask how thinking is related to percept. It makes no difference whether or no the percept, in the shape given to me, exists continuously before and after my forming a mental picture; if I want to assert anything whatever about it, I can do so only with the help of thinking. If I assert that the world is my mental picture, I have enunciated the result of an act of thinking, and if my thinking is not applicable to the world, then this result is false. Between a percept and every kind of assertion about it there intervenes thinking.

The reason why we generally overlook thinking in our consideration of things has already been given (see page 26). It lies in the fact that our attention is concentrated only on the object we are thinking about, but not at the same time on the thinking itself. The naïve consciousness, therefore, treats thinking as something which has nothing to do with things, but stands altogether aloof from them and contemplates them. The picture which the thinker makes of the phenomena of the world is regarded not as something belonging to the things but as existing only in the human head. The world is complete in itself without this picture. It is finished and complete with all its substances and forces, and of this ready-made world man makes a picture. Whoever thinks thus need only be asked one question. What right have you to declare the world to be complete without thinking? Does not the world produce thinking in the heads of men with the same necessity as it produces the blossom on a plant? Plant a seed in the earth. It puts forth root and stem, it unfolds into leaves and blossoms. Set the plant before yourself. It connects itself, in your mind, with a definite concept. Why should this concept belong any less to the whole plant than leaf and blossom? You say the leaves and blossoms exist quite apart from a perceiving subject, but the concept appears only when a human being confronts the plant. Quite so. But leaves and blossoms also appear on the plant only if there is soil in which the seed can be planted, and light and air in which the leaves and blossoms can unfold. Just so the concept of a plant arises when a thinking consciousness approaches the plant.

It is quite arbitrary to regard the sum of what we experience of a thing through bare perception as a totality, as the whole thing, while that which reveals itself through *thoughtful contemplation* is regarded as a mere accretion which has nothing to do with the thing itself. If I am given a rosebud today, the picture that offers itself to my perception is complete only for the moment. If I put the bud into water, I shall tomorrow get a very different picture of my object. If I watch the rosebud without interruption, I shall see today's state change continuously into tomorrow's through an infinite number of intermediate stages. The picture which presents itself to me at any one moment is only a chance cross-section of an object which is in a continual process of development. If I do not put the bud into water, a whole series of states which lay as *possibilities* within the bud will not develop. Similarly I may be prevented tomorrow from observing the blossom further, and will thereby have an incomplete picture of it.

It would be a quite unobjective and fortuitous kind of opinion that declared of the purely momentary appearance of a thing: *this* is the thing.

Just as little is it legitimate to regard the sum of perceptual characteristics as the thing. It might be quite possible for a spirit to receive the concept at the same time as, and united with, the percept. It would never occur to such a spirit that the concept did not belong to the thing. It would have to

66

ascribe to the concept an existence indivisibly bound up with the thing.

I will make myself clearer by an example. If I throw a stone horizontally through the air, I perceive it in different places one after the other. I connect these places so as to form a line. Mathematics teaches me to know various kinds of lines, one of which is the parabola. I know the parabola to be a line which is produced when a point moves according to a particular law. If I examine the conditions under which the stone thrown by me moves, I find the path traversed is identical with the line I know as a parabola. That the stone moves just in a parabola is a result of the given conditions and follows necessarily from them. The form of the parabola belongs to the whole phenomenon as much as any other feature of it does. The spirit described above who has no need of the detour of thinking would find itself presented not only with a sequence of visual percepts at different points but, as part and parcel of these phenomena, also with the parabolic form of the path which *we* add to the phenomenon only by thinking.

It is not due to the objects that they are given to us at first without their corresponding concepts, but to our mental organization. Our whole being functions in such a way that from every real thing the relevant elements come to us from two sides, from *perceiving* and from *thinking*.

The way I am organized for apprehending the things has nothing to do with the nature of the things themselves. The gap between perceiving and thinking exists only from the moment that I as spectator confront the things. Which elements do, and which do not, belong to the things cannot depend at all on the manner in which I obtain my knowledge of these elements.

Man is a limited being. First of all, he is a being among

other beings. His existence belongs to space and time. Thus only a limited part of the total universe can be given to him at any one time. This limited part, however, is linked up with other parts in all directions both in time and in space. If our existence were so linked up with the things that every occurrence in the world were at the same time also an occurrence in *us*, the distinction between ourselves and the things would not exist. But then there would be no separate things at all for us. All occurrences would pass continuously one into another. The cosmos would be a unity and a whole, complete in itself. The stream of events would nowhere be interrupted. It is owing to our limitations that a thing appears to us as single and separate when in truth it is not a separate thing at all. Nowhere, for example, is the single quality "red" to be found by itself in isolation. It is surrounded on all sides by other qualities to which it belongs, and without which it could not subsist. For us, however, it is necessary to isolate certain sections of the world and to consider them by themselves. Our eye can grasp only single colours one after another out of a manifold totality of colour, and our understanding can grasp only single concepts out of a connected conceptual system. This separating off is a subjective act, which is due to the fact that we are not identical with the world process, but are a single being among other beings.

The all important thing now is to determine how the being that we ourselves are is related to the other entities. This determination must be distinguished from merely becoming conscious of ourselves. For this latter self-awareness we depend on perceiving just as we do for our awareness of any other thing. The perception of myself reveals to me a number of qualities which I combine into my personality as a whole, just as I combine the qualities yellow, metallic, hard, etc., in the unity "gold". The perception of myself does not take me beyond the sphere of what belongs to me. This perceiving of myself must be distinguished from determining myself by means of *thinking*. Just as, by means of thinking, I fit any single external percept into the whole world context, so by means of thinking I integrate into the world process the percepts I have made of myself. My self-perception confines me within definite limits, but my thinking is not concerned with these limits. In this sense I am a two-sided being. I am enclosed within the sphere which I perceive as that of my personality, but I am also the bearer of an activity which, from a higher sphere, defines my limited existence. Our thinking is not individual like our sensing and feeling; it is universal. It receives an individual stamp in each separate human being only because it comes to be related to his individual feelings and sensations. By means of these particular colourings of the universal thinking, individual men differentiate themselves from one another. There is only one single concept of "triangle". It is quite immaterial for the content of this concept whether it is grasped in A's consciousness or in B's. It will, however, be grasped by each of the two in his own individual way.

This thought is opposed by a common prejudice very hard to overcome. This prejudice prevents one from seeing that the concept of a triangle that my head grasps is the same as the concept that my neighbour's head grasps. The naïve man believes himself to be the creator of his concepts. Hence he believes that each person has his own concepts. It is a fundamental requirement of philosophic thinking that it should overcome this prejudice. The one uniform concept of "triangle" does not become a multiplicity because it is thought by many persons. For the thinking of the many is in itself a unity.

In thinking we have that element given us which welds our separate individuality into one whole with the cosmos. In so far as we sense and feel (and also perceive), we are single beings; in so far as we think, we are the all-one being that pervades everything. This is the deeper meaning of our two-sided nature: We see coming into being in us a force complete and absolute in itself, a force which is universal but which we learn to know, not as it issues from the centre of the world, but rather at a point in the periphery. Were we to know it at its source, we should understand the whole riddle of the universe the moment we became conscious. But since we stand at a point in the periphery, and find that our own existence is bounded by definite limits, we must explore the region which lies outside our own being with the help of thinking which projects into us from the universal world existence.

The fact that thinking, in us, reaches out beyond our separate existence and relates itself to the universal world existence, gives rise to the fundamental desire for knowledge in us. Beings without thinking do not have this desire. When they are faced with other things no questions arise for them. These other things remain external to such beings. But in thinking beings the concept rises up when they confront the external thing. It is that part of the thing which we receive not from without but from within. To match up, to unite the two elements, inner and outer, is the task of *knowledge*.

The percept is thus not something finished and self-contained, but only one side of the total reality. The other side is the concept. The act of knowing is the synthesis of percept and concept. Only the percept and concept together constitute the whole thing.

The foregoing arguments show that it is senseless to look for any common element in the separate entities of the world other than the ideal content that thinking offers us. All attempts to find a unity in the world other than this internally coherent ideal content, which we gain by a thoughtful contemplation of our percepts, are bound to fail. Neither a humanly personal God, nor force, nor matter, nor the blind will (Schopenhauer), can be valid for us as a universal world unity. All these entities belong only to limited spheres of our observation. Humanly limited personality we perceive only in ourselves; force and matter in external things. As far as the will is concerned, it can be regarded only as the expression of the activity of our finite personality. Schopenhauer wants to avoid making "abstract" thinking the bearer of unity in the world, and seeks instead something which presents itself to him immediately as real. This philosopher believes that we can never approach the world so long as we regard it as "external" world.

In point of fact, the sought-for meaning of the world which confronts me as nothing more than my mental picture, or the passage from the world as mere mental picture of the knowing subject to whatever else it may be besides this, could never be found at all if the investigator himself were nothing more than the purely knowing subject (a winged cherub without a body). But he himself is rooted in that world: he finds himself in it as an *individual*, that is to say, his knowledge, which is the determining factor supporting the whole world as mental picture, is thus always given though the medium of a body whose affections are, for the intellect, the starting point for the contemplation of that world, as we have shown. For the purely knowing subject as such, this body is a mental picture like any other, an object among objects: its movements and actions are so far known to him in precisely the same way as the changes of all other perceived objects, and would be just as strange and incomprehensible to him if their sense were not made clear for him in an entirely different way. . . . To the subject of knowledge, who appears as an individual through his identity with the body, this body is given in two entirely different ways: once as a mental picture for intelligent contemplation, as an object among objects and obeying their laws; but at the same time, in quite a different way, namely as the thing immediately known to everyone by the word *will.* Every true act of his will is at once and without exception also a movement of his body: he cannot will the act without at the same time perceiving that it appears as a movement of the body. The act of will and the action of the body are not two things objectively known to be different which the bond of causality unites; they do not stand in the relation of cause and effect; they are one and the same, but they are given in two entirely different ways: once quite directly and once in contemplation for the intellect.*

Schopenhauer considers himself entitled by these arguments to find in the human body the "objectivity" of the will. He believes that in the activities of the body he feels an *immediate* reality—the thing-in-itself in the concrete. Against these arguments it must be said that the activities of our body come to our consciousness only through percepts of the self, and that, as such, they are in no way superior to other percepts. If we want to *know* their real nature, we can do so only by a *thinking* investigation, that is, by fitting them into the ideal system of our concepts and ideas.

Rooted most deeply in the naïve consciousness is the opinion that thinking is abstract, without any concrete content; it can at most give us an "ideal" counterpart of the unity of the world, but never that unity itself. Whoever judges in this way has never made it clear to himself what a percept without a concept really is. Let us see what this world of percepts is like: a mere juxtaposition in space, a mere succession in time, a mass of unconnected details—

* *Die Welt als Wille und Vorstellung*, Book 2, par. 18.

that is how it appears. None of the things which come and go on the stage of perception has any direct connection, that can be perceived, with any other. The world is thus a multiplicity of objects of equal value. None plays any greater part in the whole machinery of the world than any other. If it is to become clear to us that this or that fact has greater significance than another, we must consult our thinking. Were thinking not to function, the rudimentary organ of an animal which has no significance in its life would appear equal in value to the most important limb of its body. The separate facts appear in their true significance, both in themselves and for the rest of the world, only when thinking spins its threads from one entity to another. This activity of thinking is one *full of content*. For it is only through a quite definite concrete content that I can know why the snail belongs to a lower level of organization than the lion. The mere appearance, the percept, gives me no content which could inform me as to the degree of perfection of the organization.

Thinking offers this content to the percept, from man's world of concepts and ideas. In contrast to the content of the percept which is given to us from without, the content of thinking appears inwardly. The form in which this first makes its appearance we will call *intuition*. *Intuition* is for thinking what *observation* is for the percept. Intuition and observation are the sources of our knowledge. An observed object of the world remains unintelligible to us until we have within ourselves the corresponding intuition which adds that part of the reality which is lacking in the percept. To anyone who is incapable of finding intuitions corresponding to the things, the full reality remains inaccessible. Just as the colour-blind person sees only differences of brightness without any colour qualities, so can the person without intuition observe only unconnected perceptual fragments.

To *explain* a thing, to *make it intelligible,* means nothing else than to place it into the context from which it has been torn by the peculiar character of our organization as already described. A thing cut off from the world-whole does not exist. All isolating has only subjective validity for our organization. For us the universe divides itself up into above and below, before and after, cause and effect, thing and mental picture, matter and force, object and subject, etc. What appears to us in observation as separate parts becomes combined, bit by bit, through the coherent, unified world of our intuitions. By thinking we fit together again into one piece all that we have taken apart through perceiving.

The enigmatic character of an object consists in its separateness. But this separation is our own making and can, within the world of concepts, be overcome again.

Except through thinking and perceiving nothing is given to us directly. The question now arises: What is the significance of the percept, according to our line of argument? We have learnt that the proof which critical idealism offers of the subjective nature of percepts collapses. But insight into the falsity of the proof is not alone sufficient to show that the doctrine itself is erroneous. Critical idealism does not base its proof on the absolute nature of thinking, but relies on the argument that naïve realism, when followed to its logical conclusion, cancels itself out. How does the matter appear when we have recognized the absoluteness of thinking?

Let us assume that a certain percept, for example, red, appears in my consciousness. To continued observation, this percept shows itself to be connected with other percepts, for example, with a definite figure and with certain tempera-

74

ture- and touch-percepts. This combination I call an object belonging to the sense-perceptible world. I can now ask myself: Over and above the percepts just mentioned, what else is there in the section of space in which they appear? I shall then find mechanical, chemical, and other processes in that section of space. I next go further and study the processes which I find on the way from the object to my sense organs. I can find movements in an elastic medium, which by their very nature have not the slightest in common with the percepts from which I started. I get the same result if I go on and examine the transmission from sense organs to brain. In each of these fields I gather new percepts, but the connecting medium which weaves through all these spatially and temporally separated percepts is *thinking*. The air vibrations which transmit sound are given to me as percepts just like the sound itself. Thinking alone links all these percepts to one another and shows them to us in their mutual relationship. We cannot speak of anything existing beyond what is directly perceived except what can be recognized through the ideal connections of percepts, that is, connections accessible to thinking. The way objects as percepts are related to the subject as percept—a relationship that goes beyond what is merely perceived—is therefore purely ideal, that is, it can be expressed only by means of concepts. Only if I could perceive how the percept *object* affects the percept *subject*, or, conversely, could watch the building up of the perceptual pattern by the subject, would it be possible to speak as modern physiology and the critical idealism based on it do. Their view confuses an ideal relation (that of the object to the subject) with a process which we could speak of only if it were possible to perceive it. The proposition, "No colour without a colour-sensing eye," cannot be taken to mean that the eye produces the colour, but only that an ideal relation, recognizable by thinking, subsists between the percept "colour" and the percept "eye". Empirical science will have to ascertain how the properties of the eye and those of the colours are related to one another, by what means the organ of sight transmits the perception of colours, and so forth. I can trace how one percept succeeds another in time and is related to others in space, and I can formulate these relations in conceptual terms, but I can never perceive how a percept originates out of the non-perceptible. All attempts to seek any relations between percepts other than thought relations must of necessity fail.

What then is a percept? The question, asked in this general way, is absurd. A percept emerges always as something perfectly definite, as a concrete content. This content is directly given and is completely contained in what is given. The only question one can ask concerning the given content is what it is apart from perception, that is, what it is for thinking. The question concerning the "what" of a percept can, therefore, only refer to the conceptual intuition that corresponds to this percept. From this point of view, the question of the subjectivity of percepts, in the sense of critical idealism, cannot be raised at all. Only what is perceived as belonging to the subject can be termed "subjective". To form a link between something subjective and something objective is impossible for any process that is "real" in the naïve sense, that is, one that can be perceived; it is possible only for thinking. Therefore what appears for our perception to be external to the percept of myself as subject is for us "objective". The percept of myself as subject remains perceptible to me after the table which now stands before me has disappeared from my field of observation. The observation of the table has produced in me a modification which likewise persists. I retain the faculty to produce later on an image of the table. This faculty of producing an image remains connected with me. Psychology calls this image a memory-picture. It is in fact the only thing that can justifiably be called the *mental picture* of the table. For it corresponds to the perceptible modification of my own state through the presence of the table in my visual field. Moreover, it does not mean a modification of some "Ego-in-itself" standing behind the percept of the subject, but the modification of the perceptible subject itself. The mental picture is, therefore, a subjective percept, in contrast with the objective percept which occurs when the object is present in the field of vision. Confusing the *subjective* percept with the *objective* percept leads to the misconception contained in idealism—that the world is my mental picture.

Our next task must be to define the concept of "mental picture" more closely. What we have said about it so far does not give us the concept of it but only shows us whereabouts in the perceptual field the mental picture is to be found. The exact concept of "mental picture" will make it possible for us also to obtain a satisfactory explanation of the way that mental picture and object are related. This will then lead us over the border line where the relationship between the human subject and the object belonging to the world is brought down from the purely conceptual field of cognition into concrete individual *life*. Once we know what to make of the world, it will be a simple matter to direct ourselves accordingly. We can only act with full energy when we know *what* it is in the world to which we devote our activity.

77

Author's addition, 1918

The view I have outlined here may be regarded as one to which man is at first quite naturally driven when he begins to reflect upon his relation to the world. He then finds himself caught in a system of thoughts which dissolves for him as fast as he frames it. The thought formation is such that it requires something more than mere theoretical refutation. We have to *live through it* in order to understand the aberration into which it leads us and thence to find the way out. It must figure in any discussion of the relation of man to the world, not for the sake of refuting others whom one believes to be holding mistaken views about this relation, but because it is necessary to understand the confusion to which every first effort at reflection about such a relation is apt to lead. One needs to arrive at just *that* insight which will enable one to refute *oneself* with respect to these first reflections. This is the point of view from which the arguments of the preceding chapter are put forward.

Whoever tries to work out for himself a view of the relation of man to the world becomes aware of the fact that he creates this relation, at least in part, by forming mental pictures about the things and events in the world. In consequence, his attention is deflected from what exists *outside* in the world and is directed towards his inner world, the life of his mental pictures. He begins to say to himself: It is impossible for me to have a relationship to any thing or event unless a mental picture appears in me. Once we have noticed this fact, it is but a step to the opinion: After all, I experience only my mental pictures; I know of a world outside me only in so far as it is a mental picture *in me.* With this opinion, the standpoint of naïve realism, which man takes up prior to all reflection about his relation to the world, is abandoned. So long as he keeps that standpoint, he believes that he is dealing with real things, but reflection about himself drives him away from it. Reflection prevents him from turning his gaze towards a real world such as naïve consciousness believes it has before it; it allows him to gaze only upon his mental pictures—*these* interpose themselves between his own being and a supposedly real world, such as the naïve point of view believes itself entitled to affirm. Man can no longer see such a real world through the intervening world of mental pictures. He must suppose that he is blind to such a reality. Thus arises the thought of a "thing-in-itself" which is inaccessible to knowledge.

So long as we consider only the relationship to the world, into which man appears to enter through the life of his mental pictures, we cannot escape from this form of thought. Yet one cannot remain at the standpoint of naïve realism except by closing one's mind artificially to the craving for knowledge. The very existence of this craving for knowledge about the relation of man to the world shows that this naïve point of view must be abandoned. If the naïve point of view yielded anything we could acknowledge as truth, we could never experience this craving.

But we do not arrive at anything else which we could regard as truth if we merely abandon the naïve point of view while unconsciously retaining the type of thought which it necessitates. This is just the mistake made by the man who says to himself, "I experience only my mental pictures, and though I believe that I am dealing with realities, I am actually conscious only of my mental pictures of realities. I must therefore suppose that the true realities, the 'things-in-themselves', exist only beyond the horizon of my consciousness, that I know absolutely nothing of them directly, and that they somehow approach me and influence me so that my world of mental pictures arises in me." Whoever thinks in this way is merely adding another world in his thoughts to the world already spread out before him. But with regard to this additional world, he ought strictly to begin his thinking activity all over again. For the unknown "thing-in-itself", in its relation to man's own nature, is conceived in exactly the same way as is the known thing in the sense of naïve realism.

One only avoids the confusion into which one falls through the critical attitude based on this naïve standpoint, if one notices that, *inside* everything we can experience by means of perceiving, be it within ourselves or outside in the world, there is *something* which cannot suffer the fate of having a mental picture interpose itself between the process and the person observing it. *This something is thinking.* With regard to thinking we *can* maintain the point of view of naïve realism. If we fail to do so, it is only because we have learnt that we must abandon it in the case of other things, but overlook that what we have found to be true for these other things does not apply to thinking. When we realize this, we open the way to the further insight that *in* thinking and *through* thinking man must recognize the very thing to which he has apparently blinded himself by having to interpose his life of mental pictures between the world and himself.

From a source greatly respected by the author of this book comes the objection that this discussion of thinking remains at the level of a naïve realism of thinking, just as one might object if someone held the real world and the world of mental pictures to be one and the same. However, the author believes himself to have shown in this very discussion that the validity of this "naïve realism" *for thinking* results inevitably from an unprejudiced observation of thinking; and that naïve realism, in so far as it is invalid for other things, is overcome through the recognition of the true nature of thinking.

CHAPTER SIX

Human Individuality

IN explaining mental pictures, philosophers have found the chief difficulty in the fact that we ourselves are not the outer things, and yet our mental pictures must have a form corresponding to the things. But on closer inspection it turns out that this difficulty does not really exist. We certainly are not the external things, but we belong together with them to one and the same world. That section of the world which I perceive to be myself as subject is permeated by the stream of the universal cosmic process. To my perception I am, in the first instance, confined within the limits bounded by my skin. But all that is contained within this skin belongs to the cosmos as a whole. Hence, for a relation to subsist between my organism and an object external to me, it is by no means necessary that something of the object should slip into me, or make an impression on my mind, like a signet ring on wax. The question: "How do I get information about that tree ten feet away from me?" is utterly misleading. It springs from the view that the boundaries of my body are absolute barriers, through which information about things filters into me. The forces which are at work inside my body are the same as those which exist outside. Therefore I really am the things; not, however, "I" in so far as I am a percept of myself as subject, but "I" in so far as I am a part of the universal world process. The percept of the tree belongs to the same whole as my I. This universal world process produces equally the percept of the tree out there and the percept of my I in here. Were I not a world knower, but world creator, object and subject (percept and I) would originate in one act. For each implies the other. In so far as these are entities that belong together, I can as world knower discover the common element in both only through thinking, which relates one to the other by means of concepts.

The most difficult to drive from the field are the so-called physiological proofs of the subjectivity of our percepts. When I exert pressure on my skin I perceive it as a pressure sensation. This same pressure can be sensed as light by the eye, as sound by the ear. An electric shock is perceived by the eye as light, by the ear as noise, by the nerves of the skin as impact, and by the nose as a phosphoric smell. What follows from these facts? Only this: I perceive an electric shock (or a pressure, as the case may be) followed by an impression of light, or sound, or perhaps a certain smell, and so on. If there were no eye present, then no perception of light would accompany the perception of the mechanical disturbance in my environment; without the presence of the ear, no perception of sound, and so on. But what right have we to say that in the absence of sense organs the whole process would not exist at all? Those who, from the fact that an electrical process calls forth light in the eye, conclude that what we sense as light is only a mechanical process of motion when outside our organism, forget that they are only passing from one percept to another, and not at all to something lying beyond percepts. Just as we can say that the eye perceives a mechanical process of motion in its surroundings as light, so we could equally well say that a regular and systematic change in an object is perceived by us as a process of motion. If I draw twelve pictures of a horse on the circumference of a rotating disc, reproducing exactly the attitudes which the horse's body successively assumes when galloping, I can produce the illusion of movement by rotating the disc. I need only look through an opening in such a way that, in the proper intervals, I see the successive positions of the horse. I do not see twelve separate pictures of a horse but the picture of a single galloping horse.

The physiological fact mentioned above cannot therefore throw any light on the relation of percept to mental picture. We must go about it rather differently.

The moment a percept appears in my field of observation, thinking also becomes active through me. An element of my thought system, a definite intuition, a concept, connects itself with the percept. Then, when the percept disappears from my field of vision, what remains? My intuition, with the reference to the particular percept which it acquired in the moment of perceiving. The degree of vividness with which I can subsequently recall this reference depends on the manner in which my mental and bodily organism is working. A *mental picture* is nothing but an intuition related to a particular percept; it is a concept that was once connected with a certain percept, and which retains the reference to this percept. My concept of a lion is not formed *out of* my percepts of lions; but my mental picture of a lion is very definitely formed according to a percept. I can convey the concept of a lion to someone who has never seen a lion. I cannot convey to him a vivid mental picture without the help of his own perception.

Thus the mental picture is an individualized concept. And now we can see how real objects can be represented to us by mental pictures. The full reality of a thing is given to us in the moment of observation through the fitting together of concept and percept. By means of a percept, the concept acquires an individualized form, a relation to this particular

84

percept. In this individualized form, which carries the reference to the percept as a characteristic feature, the concept lives on in us and constitutes the mental picture of the thing in question. If we come across a second thing with which the same concept connects itself, we recognize the second as belonging to the same kind as the first; if we come across the same thing a second time, we find in our conceptual system, not merely a corresponding concept, but the individualized concept with its characteristic relation to the same object, and thus we recognize the object again.

Thus the mental picture stands between percept and concept. It is the particularized concept which points to the percept.

The sum of those things about which I can form mental pictures may be called my total *experience*. The man who has the greater number of individualized concepts will be the man of richer experience. A man who lacks all power of intuition is not capable of acquiring experience. He loses the objects again when they disappear from his field of vision, because he lacks the concepts which he should bring into relation with them. A man whose faculty of thinking is well developed, but whose perception functions badly owing to his clumsy sense organs, will just as little be able to gather experience. He can, it is true, acquire concepts by one means or another; but his intuitions lack the vivid reference to definite things. The unthinking traveller and the scholar living in abstract conceptual systems are alike incapable of acquiring a rich sum of experience.

Reality shows itself to us as percept and concept; the subjective representative of this reality shows itself to us as *mental picture*.

If our personality expressed itself only in cognition, the

totality of all that is objective would be given in percept, concept and mental picture.

However, we are not satisfied merely to refer the percept, by means of thinking, to the concept, but we relate them also to our particular subjectivity, our individual Ego. The expression of this individual relationship is feeling, which manifests itself as pleasure or displeasure.

Thinking and *feeling* correspond to the two-fold nature of our being to which reference has already been made. *Thinking* is the element through which we take part in the universal cosmic process; *feeling* is that through which we can withdraw ourselves into the narrow confines of our own being.

Our thinking links us to the world; our feeling leads us back into ourselves and thus makes us individuals. Were we merely thinking and perceiving beings, our whole life would flow along in monotonous indifference. Were we able merely to *know* ourselves as selves, we should be totally indifferent to ourselves. It is only because we experience self-feeling with self-knowledge, and pleasure and pain with the perception of objects, that we live as individual beings whose existence is not limited to the conceptual relations between us and the rest of the world, but who have besides this a special value for ourselves.

One might be tempted to see in the life of feeling an element that is more richly saturated with reality than is the contemplation of the world through thinking. But the reply to this is that the life of feeling, after all, has this richer meaning only for my individual self. For the universe as a whole my life of feeling can have value only if, as a percept of my self, the feeling enters into connection with a concept and in this roundabout way links itself to the cosmos.

Our life is a continual oscillation between living with the

universal world process and being our own individual selves. The farther we ascend into the universal nature of thinking where in the end what is individual interests us only as an example or specimen of the concept, the more the character of the separate being, of the quite definite single personality, becomes lost in us. The farther we descend into the depths of our own life and allow our feelings to resound with our experiences of the outer world, the more we cut ourselves off from universal being. A true individuality will be the one who reaches up with his feelings to the farthest possible extent into the region of the ideal. There are men in whom even the most general ideas that enter their heads still bear that peculiar personal tinge which shows unmistakably the connection with their author. There are others whose concepts come before us without the least trace of individual character as if they had not been produced by a man of flesh and blood at all.

Making mental pictures gives our conceptual life at once an individual stamp. Each one of us has his own particular place from which he surveys the world. His concepts link themselves to his percepts. He thinks the general concepts in his own special way. This special determination results for each of us from the place where we stand in the world, from the range of percepts peculiar to our place in life.

Distinct from this determination is another which depends on our particular organization. Our organization is indeed a special, fully determined entity. Each of us combines special feelings, and these in the most varying degrees of intensity, with his percepts. This is just the individual element in the personality of each one of us. It is what remains over when we have allowed fully for all the determining factors in our surroundings.

A life of feeling, wholly devoid of thinking, would gradually lose all connection with the world. But man is meant to be a whole, and for him knowledge of *things* will go hand in hand with the development and education of the life of feeling.

Feeling is the means whereby, in the first instance, concepts gain concrete *life*.

CHAPTER SEVEN

Are There Limits to Knowledge?

WE have established that the elements for the explanation of
reality are to be found in the two spheres: perceiving and
thinking. It is due, as we have seen, to our organization that
the full, complete reality, including our own selves as
subjects, appears at first as a duality. The act of knowing
overcomes this duality by fusing the two elements of reality,
the percept and the concept gained by thinking, into the
complete thing. Let us call the manner in which the world
presents itself to us, before it has taken on its true nature
through our knowing it, "the world of appearance," in
contrast to the unified whole composed of percept and concept. We can then say: The world is given to us as a duality,
and knowledge transforms it into a unity. A philosophy
which starts from this basic principle may be called a
monistic philosophy, or *monism*. Opposed to this is the two-
world theory, or *dualism*. The latter does not assume just
that there are two sides of a single reality which are kept
apart merely by our organization, but that there are two
worlds absolutely distinct from one another. It then tries to
find in one of these two worlds the principles for the explanation of the other.

Dualism rests on a false conception of what we call knowledge. It divides the whole of existence into two spheres,
each of which has its own laws, and it leaves these two worlds
standing apart and opposed.

It is from a dualism such as this that there arises the
distinction between the perceptual object and the thing-in-

itself, which Kant introduced into philosophy, and which, to the present day, we have not succeeded in eradicating. According to our line of argument, it is due to the nature of our mental organization that a particular thing can be given to us only as a percept. Thinking then overcomes this particularity by assigning to each percept its rightful place in the world as a whole. As long as we designate the separated parts of the world as percepts, we are simply following, in this separating out, a law of our subjectivity. If, however, we regard the sum of all percepts as the one part, and contrast with this a second part, namely, the things-in-themselves, then we are philosophizing into the blue. We are merely playing with concepts. We construct an artificial pair of opposites, but we can gain no content for the second of these opposites, since such content for a particular thing can be drawn only from perception.

Every kind of existence that is assumed outside the realm of percept and concept must be relegated to the sphere of unjustified hypotheses. To this category belongs the "thing-in-itself". It is quite natural that a dualistic thinker should be unable to find the connection between the world principle which he hypothetically assumes and the things given in experience. A *content* for the hypothetical world principle can be arrived at only by borrowing it from the world of experience and then shutting one's eyes to the fact of the borrowing. Otherwise it remains an empty concept, a non-concept which has nothing but the form of a concept. Here the dualistic thinker usually asserts that the content of this concept is inaccessible to our knowledge; we can know only *that* such a content exists, but not *what* it is that exists. In both cases it is impossible to overcome dualism. Even though one were to import a few abstract elements from the world of experience into the concept of the thing-in-itself, it would still remain impossible to derive the rich concrete life of experience from these few qualities which are, after all, themselves taken from perception. Du Bois-Reymond considers that the imperceptible atoms of matter produce sensation and feeling by means of their position and motion, and then comes to the conclusion that we can never find a satisfactory explanation of how matter and motion produce sensation and feeling, for "it is absolutely and for ever incomprehensible that it should be other than indifferent to a number of atoms of carbon, hydrogen, nitrogen, and so on, how they lie and move, how they lay and moved, or how they will lie and will move. It is impossible to see how consciousness could come into existence through their interaction." This conclusion is characteristic of this whole trend of thought. Position and motion are abstracted from the rich world of percepts. They are then transferred to the notional world of atoms. And then astonishment arises that real life cannot be evolved out of this self-made principle borrowed from the world of percepts.

That the dualist can reach no explanation of the world, working as he does with a completely empty concept of the "in-itself" of a thing, follows at once from the very definition of his principle given above.

In every case the dualist finds himself compelled to set impassable barriers to our faculty of knowledge. The follower of a monistic world conception knows that everything he needs for the explanation of any given phenomenon in the world must lie within this world itself. What prevents him from reaching it can be only accidental limitations in space and time, or defects of his organization, that is, not of human organization in general, but only of his own particular one.

It follows from the concept of the act of knowing as we

have defined it, that one cannot speak of limits to knowledge. Knowing is not a concern of the world in general, but an affair which man must settle for himself. *Things* demand no explanation. They exist and act on one another according to laws which can be discovered through thinking. They exist in indivisible unity with these laws. Our Egohood confronts them, grasping at first only that part of them we have called percepts. Within our Egohood, however, lies the power to discover the other part of the reality as well. Only when the Egohood has taken the two elements of reality which are indivisibly united in the world and has combined them also for itself, is our thirst for knowledge satisfied—the I has then arrived at the reality once more.

Thus the conditions necessary for an act of knowledge to take place are there *through* the I and *for* the I. The I sets itself the problems of knowledge; and moreover it takes them from an element that is absolutely clear and transparent in itself: the element of thinking. If we set ourselves questions which we cannot answer, it must be because the content of the questions is not in all respects clear and distinct. It is not the world which sets us the questions, but we ourselves.

I can imagine that it would be quite impossible for me to answer a question which I happened to find written down somewhere, without knowing the sphere from which the content of the question was taken.

In our knowledge we are concerned with questions which arise for us through the fact that a sphere of percepts, conditioned by place, time, and our subjective organization, is confronted by a sphere of concepts pointing to the totality of the universe. My task consists in reconciling these two spheres, with both of which I am well acquainted. Here one cannot speak of a limit to knowledge. It may be that, at any particular moment, this or that remains unexplained because, through our place in life, we are prevented from perceiving the things involved. What is not found today, however, may be found tomorrow. The limits due to these causes are only transitory, and can be overcome by the progress of perception and thinking.

Dualism makes the mistake of transferring the antithesis of object and subject, which has meaning only within the perceptual realm, to purely notional entities outside this realm. But since the separate things within the perceptual field remain separated only so long as the perceiver refrains from thinking (which cancels all separation and shows it to be due to purely subjective factors), the dualist is therefore transferring to entities behind the perceptible realm determining factors which even for this realm have no absolute validity, but only relative. He thus splits up the two factors concerned in the process of knowledge, namely percept and concept, into four: (1) the object in itself; (2) the precept which the subject has of the object; (3) the subject; (4) the concept which relates the precept to the object in itself. The relation between subject and object is a *real* one; the subject is really (dynamically) influenced by the object. This real process is said not to appear in consciousness. But it is supposed to evoke in the subject a response to the stimulation from the object. The result of this response is said to be the percept. Only at this stage does it enter our consciousness. The object is said to have an objective (independent of the subject) reality, the percept a subjective reality. This subjective reality is referred by the subject to the object. This reference is called an *ideal* one. With this the dualist therefore splits up the process of knowledge into two parts. The one part, namely, the production of the perceptual object out of the thing-in-itself, he conceives of as taking place *outside consciousness*, whereas the other, the combination of percept with concept and the reference of the concept to the object, takes place, according to him, *within consciousness*.

With these presuppositions, it is clear why the dualist believes his concepts to be merely subjective representatives of what is there *prior* to his consciousness. The objectively real process in the subject by means of which the percept comes about, and still more the objective relations between things-in-themselves, remain for such a dualist inaccessible to direct knowledge; according to him, man can obtain only conceptual representatives of the objectively real. The bond of unity which connects things with one another and also objectively with the individual mind of each of us (as thing-in-itself) lies beyond our consciousness in a being-in-itself of whom, once more, we can have in our consciousness merely a conceptual representative.

The dualist believes that he would dissolve away the whole world into a mere abstract scheme of concepts, did he not insist on *real* connections between the objects besides the conceptual ones. In other words, the ideal principles which thinking discovers seem too airy for the dualist, and he seeks, in addition, real principles with which to support them.

Let us examine these real principles a little more closely. The naïve man (naïve realist) regards the objects of external experience as realities. The fact that his hands can grasp these objects, and his eyes see them, is for him sufficient proof of their reality. "Nothing exists that cannot be perceived" is, in fact, the first axiom of the naïve man; and it is held to be equally valid in its converse: "Everything which can be perceived exists." The best evidence for this assertion is the naïve man's belief in immortality and ghosts. He thinks of the soul as refined material substance which may, in special circumstances, become visible even to the ordinary man (naïve belief in ghosts).

In contrast with this real world of his, the naïve realist regards everything else, especially the world of ideas, as unreal or "merely ideal". What we add to objects by thinking is nothing more than thoughts *about* the things. Thought adds nothing real to the percept.

But it is not only with reference to the existence of *things* that the naïve man regards sense perception as the sole proof of reality, but also with reference to events. A thing, according to him, can act on another only when a force actually present to sense perception issues from the one and seizes upon the other. In the older physics it was thought that very fine substances emanate from the objects and penetrate through the sense organs into the soul. The actual seeing of these substances is impossible only because of the coarseness of our sense organs relative to the fineness of these substances. In principle, the reason for attributing reality to these substances was the same as for attributing it to the objects of the sense-perceptible world, namely because of their mode of existence, which was thought to be analogous to that of sense-perceptible reality.

The self-contained nature of what can be experienced through ideas is not regarded by the naïve mind as being real in the same way that sense experience is. An object grasped in "mere idea" is regarded as a chimera until conviction of its reality can be given through sense perception. In short, the naïve man demands the real evidence of his senses in addition to the ideal evidence of his thinking. In this need of the naïve man lies the original ground for primitive forms of the belief in revelation. The God who is given through thinking remains to the naïve mind always a merely *"notional"*

God. The naïve mind demands a manifestation that is accessible to sense perception. God must appear in the flesh, and little value is attached to the testimony of thinking, but only to proof of divinity such as changing water into wine in a way that can be testified by the senses.

Even the act of knowing itself is pictured by the naïve man as a process analogous to sense perception. Things, it is thought, make an *impression* on the soul, or send out images which enter through our senses, and so on.

What the naïve man can perceive with his senses he regards as real, and what he cannot thus perceive (God, soul, knowledge, etc.) he regards as analogous to what he does perceive.

A science based on naïve realism would have to be nothing but an exact *description* of the content of perception. For naïve realism, concepts are only the means to an end. They exist to provide ideal counterparts of percepts, and have no significance for the things themselves. For the naïve realist, only the individual tulips which he sees (or could see) are real; the single idea of the tulip is to him an abstraction, the unreal thought-picture which the soul has put together out of the characteristics common to all tulips.

Naïve realism, with its fundamental principle of the reality of all perceived things, is contradicted by experience, which teaches us that the content of percepts is of a transitory nature. The tulip I see is real today; in a year it will have vanished into nothingness. What persists is the *species* tulip. For the naïve realist, however, this species is *"only"* an *idea*, not a reality. Thus this theory of the world find itself in the position of seeing its realities arise and perish, while what it regards as unreal, in contrast with the real, persists. Hence naïve realism is compelled to acknowledge, in addition to percepts, the existence of something ideal. It must admit entities which cannot be perceived by the senses. In doing so, it justifies itself by conceiving their existence as being analogous to that of sense-perceptible objects. Just such hypothetical realities are the invisible forces by means of which the sense-perceptible objects act on one another. Another such thing is heredity, which works on beyond the individual and is the reason why a new being which develops from the individual is similar to it, thereby serving to maintain the species. Such a thing again is the life-principle permeating the organic body, the soul for which the naïve mind always finds a concept formed in analogy with sense realities, and finally the naïve man's Divine Being. This Divine Being is thought of as acting in a manner exactly corresponding to the way in which man himself is *seen* to act; that is, anthropomorphically.

Modern physics traces sensations back to processes of the smallest particles of bodies and of an infinitely fine substance, called ether, or to other such things. For example, what we experience as warmth is, within the space occupied by the warmth-giving body, the movement of its parts. Here again something imperceptible is conceived in analogy with what is perceptible. In this sense, the perceptual analogue to the concept "body" would be, shall we say, the interior of a totally enclosed space, in which elastic spheres are moving in all directions, impinging one on another, bouncing on and off the walls, and so on.*

Without such assumptions the world would fall apart for the naïve realist into an incoherent aggregate of percepts without mutual relationships and with no tendency to unite.

* That is, movements of a kind similar to those which *can* be perceived are supposed to occur *imperceptibly* within the body and to account for the warmth which is perceived directly but as something quite different.—*Translator's footnote.*

97

It is clear, however, that naïve realism can make these assumptions only by an inconsistency. If it would remain true to its fundamental principle that only what is perceived is real, then it ought not to assume a reality where it perceives nothing. The imperceptible forces which proceed from the perceptible things are in fact unjustified hypotheses from the standpoint of naïve realism. And because naïve realism knows no other realities, it invests its hypothetical forces with perceptual content. It thus ascribes a form of existence (perceptible existence) to a sphere where the only means of making any assertion about such existence, namely, sense perception, is lacking.

This self-contradictory theory leads to metaphysical realism. This constructs, in addition to the perceptible reality, an imperceptible reality which it conceives on the analogy of the perceptible one. Therefore metaphysical realism is of necessity dualistic.

Wherever the metaphysical realist observes a relationship between perceptible things (such as when two things move towards each other, or when something objective enters consciousness), there he sees a reality. However, the relationship which he notices can only be expressed by means of thinking; it cannot be perceived. The purely ideal relationship is then arbitrarily made into something similar to a perceptible one. Thus, according to this theory, the real world is composed of the objects of perception which are in ceaseless flux, arising and disappearing, and of imperceptible forces which produce the objects of perception, and are the things that endure.

Metaphysical realism is a contradictory mixture of naïve realism and idealism. Its hypothetical forces are imperceptible entities endowed with the qualities of percepts. The metaphysical realist has made up his mind to acknowledge, in addition to the sphere which he is able to know through perception, another sphere for which this means of knowledge fails him and which can be known only by means of thinking. But he cannot make up his mind at the same time to acknowledge that the mode of existence which thinking reveals, namely, the concept (idea), is just as important a factor as the percept. If we are to avoid the contradiction of imperceptible percepts, we must admit that the relationships which thinking establishes between the percepts can have no other mode of existence for us than that of concepts. If we reject the untenable part of metaphysical realism, the world presents itself to us as the sum of percepts and their conceptual (ideal) relationships. Metaphysical realism would then merge into a view of the world which requires the principle of perceivability for percepts and that of conceivability for the relationships between the percepts. This view of the world can admit no third sphere—in addition to the world of percepts and the world of concepts—in which both the so-called "real" and "ideal" principles are simultaneously valid.

When the metaphysical realist asserts that, besides the ideal relationship between the percept of the object and the percept of the subject, there must also exist a real relationship between the "thing-in-itself" of the percept and the "thing-in-itself" of the perceptible subject (that is, of the so-called individual spirit), he is basing his assertion on the false assumption of a real process, analogous to the processes in the sense world but imperceptible. Further, when the metaphysical realist asserts that we enter into a conscious ideal relationship to our world of percepts, but that to the real world we can have only a dynamic (force) relationship, he repeats the mistake we have already criticized. One can

99

talk of a dynamic relationship only within the world of percepts (in the sphere of the sense of touch), but not outside that world.

Let us call the view which we have characterized above, into which metaphysical realism merges when it discards its contradictory elements, *monism*, because it combines one-sided realism with idealism into a higher unity.

For naïve realism, the real world is an aggregate of perceived objects (percepts); for metaphysical realism, not only percepts but also imperceptible forces are real; monism replaces forces by ideal connections which are gained through thinking. The *laws of nature* are just such connections. A law of nature is in fact nothing but the conceptual expression of the connection between certain percepts.

Monism never finds it necessary to ask for any principles of explanation for reality other than percepts and concepts. It knows that in the whole field of reality there is *no occasion* for this question. In the perceptual world, as it presents itself directly to perception, it sees one half of the reality; in the union of this world with the world of concepts it finds the full reality.

The metaphysical realist may object to the adherent of monism: It may be that for your organization, your knowledge is complete in itself, with no part lacking; but you do not know how the world is mirrored in an intelligence organized differently from your own. To this the monist will reply: If there are intelligences other than human, and if their percepts are different from ours, all that concerns me is what reaches me from them through perception and concept. Through my perceiving, that is, through this specifically human mode of perceiving, I, as subject, am confronted with the object. The connection of things is thereby interrupted. The subject restores this connection by means of thinking. In doing so it puts itself back into the context of the world as a whole. Since it is only through the subject that the whole appears cut in two at the place between our percept and our concept, the uniting of those two gives us true knowledge. For beings with a different perceptual world (for example, if they had twice our number of sense organs), the continuum would appear broken in another place, and the reconstruction would accordingly have to take a form specific for such beings. The question concerning the limits of knowledge exists only for naïve and metaphysical realism, both of which see in the contents of the soul only an ideal representation of the real world. For these theories, what exists *outside* the subject is something absolute, founded in itself, and what is contained *within* the subject is a picture of this absolute, but quite external to it. The completeness of knowledge depends on the greater or lesser degree of resemblance between the picture and the absolute object. A being with fewer senses than man will perceive less of the world, one with more senses will perceive more. The former will accordingly have a less complete knowledge than the latter.

For monism, the situation is different. The manner in which the world continuum appears to be rent asunder into subject and object depends on the organization of the perceiving being. The object is not absolute, but merely relative, with reference to this particular subject. Bridging over the antithesis, therefore, can again take place only in the quite specific way that is characteristic of the particular human subject. As soon as the I, which is separated from the world in the act of perceiving, fits itself back into the world continuum through thoughtful contemplation, all further questioning ceases, having been but a consequence of the separation.

A differently constituted being would have a differently constituted knowledge. Our own knowledge suffices to answer the questions put by our own nature.

Metaphysical realism has to ask: By what means are our percepts given? What is it that affects the subject?

Monism holds that percepts are determined through the subject. But at the same time, the subject has in thinking the means for cancelling this self-produced determination.

The metaphysical realist is faced by a further difficulty when he seeks to explain the similarity between the world pictures of different human individuals. He has to ask himself: How is it that the picture of the world which I build up out of my subjectively determined percepts and my concepts turns out to be the same as the one which another individual is also building up out of the same two subjective factors? How can I, in any case, draw conclusions from my own subjective picture of the world about that of another human being? The fact that people can understand and get on with one another in practical life leads the metaphysical realist to conclude that their subjective world pictures must be similar. From the similarity of these world pictures he then further concludes that the "individual spirits" behind the single human subjects as percepts, or the "I-in-itself" behind the subjects, must also be like one another.

This is an inference from a sum of effects to the character of the underlying causes. We believe that we can understand the situation well enough from a sufficiently large number of instances to know how the inferred causes will behave in other instances. Such an inference is called an inductive inference. We shall be obliged to modify its results if further observation yields some unexpected element, because the character of our conclusion is, after all, determined only by the particular form of our actual observations. The metaphysical realist asserts that this knowledge of causes, though conditional, is nevertheless quite sufficient for practical life.

Inductive inference is the method underlying modern metaphysical realism. At one time it was thought that we could evolve something out of concepts that is no longer a concept. It was thought that the metaphysical realities, which metaphysical realism after all requires, could be known by means of concepts. This kind of philosophizing is now out of date. Instead it is thought that one can infer from a sufficiently large number of perceptual facts the character of the thing-in-itself which underlies these facts. Whereas formerly it was from concepts, now it is from percepts that people seek to evolve the metaphysical. Since one has concepts before oneself in transparent clearness, it was thought that one might be able to deduce the metaphysical from them with absolute certainty. Percepts are not given with the same transparent clearness. Each subsequent one is a little different from others of the same kind which preceded it. Basically, therefore, anything inferred from past percepts will be somewhat modified by each subsequent percept. The character of the metaphysical thus obtained can, therefore, be only relatively true, since it is subject to correction by further instances. Eduard von Hartmann's metaphysics has a character determined by this basic method, as expressed in the motto on the title page of his first important book: "Speculative results following the inductive method of Natural Science."

The form which the metaphysical realist nowadays gives to his things-in-themselves is obtained by inductive inferences.

Through considerations of the process of knowledge he is convinced of the existence of an objectively real world continuum, over and above the "subjective" world continuum which we know through percepts and concepts. The nature of this reality he thinks he can determine by inductive inferences from his percepts.

Author's addition, 1918

For the unprejudiced observation of what is experienced through percept and concept, as we have tried to describe it in the foregoing pages, certain ideas which originate in the field of natural science are repeatedly found to be disturbing. Thus it is said that in the spectrum of light the eye perceives colours from red to violet. But in the space beyond the violet there are forces of radiation for which there is no corresponding colour-perception in the eye, but instead there is a definite chemical effect; in the same way, beyond the limit of the red there are radiations having only an effect of warmth. By studying these and other similar phenomena, one is led to the view that the range of man's perceptual world is determined by the range of his senses, and that he would be confronted by a very different world if he had additional, or altogether different, senses. Anyone who chooses to indulge in the extravagant flights of fancy for which the brilliant discoveries of recent scientific research offer such tempting opportunities, may well arrive at the conclusion that nothing enters man's field of observation except what can affect the senses which his bodily organization has evolved. He has no right to regard what is perceived, limited as it is by his organization, as in any way setting a standard for reality. Every new sense would confront him with a different picture of reality.

Within its proper limits this view is entirely justified. But if anyone allows this view to confuse him in his unprejudiced observation of the relationship of percept and concept as set out in these chapters, then he will bar his own way to any realistic knowledge of man and of the world. To experience the essential nature of thinking, that is, to work one's way into the world of concepts through one's own activity, is an entirely different thing from experiencing something perceptible through the senses. Whatever senses man might possibly have, not one would give him reality if his thinking did not permeate with concepts whatever he perceived by means of it. And every sense, however constructed, would, if thus permeated, enable him to live within reality. This question of how he stands in the world of reality is untouched by any speculations he may have as to how the perceptual world might appear to him if he had different senses. We must clearly understand that *every* perceptual picture of the world owes its form to the organization of the perceiving being, but also that the perceptual picture which has been thoroughly permeated by the experience of thinking leads us into *reality*. What causes us to enquire into our relationship to the world is not the fanciful pictures of how different the world would appear to other than human senses, but the realization that *every* percept gives us only a part of the reality concealed within it, in other words, that it directs us away from its *inherent* reality. Added to this is the further realization that thinking leads us into that part of the reality which the percept conceals within itself.

Another difficulty in the way of the unprejudiced observation of the relationship between the percept and the concept wrought by thinking, as here described, arises when, for example, in the field of experimental physics it becomes necessary to speak not of immediately perceptible elements, but of non-perceptible quantities as in the case of lines of electric or magnetic force. It may *seem* as if the elements of reality of which physicists speak had no connection either with what is perceptible or with the concepts which active thinking has wrought. Yet such a view would be based on self-deception. The main point is that *all* the results of physical research, apart from unjustifiable hypotheses which ought to be excluded, have been obtained through percept and concept. Elements which are seemingly non-perceptible are placed by the physicist's sound instinct for knowledge into the field where percepts lie, and they are thought of in terms of concepts commonly used in this field. The strengths of electric or magnetic fields and such like are arrived at, in the very nature of things, by no other process of knowledge than the one which occurs between percept and concept.

An increase or a modification of human senses would yield a different perceptual picture, an enrichment or a modification of human experience. But even with *this* experience one could arrive at real knowledge only through the interplay of concept and percept. The *deepening* of knowledge depends on the powers of intuition which express themselves in thinking (see page 73). In the *living experience* which develops within thinking, this intuition may dive down to greater or to lesser depths of reality. An extension of the perceptual picture may provide stimulation for this diving down of intuition, and thus indirectly promote it. But *under no circumstances* should this diving into the depths to reach reality be confused with being confronted by a perceptual picture of greater or lesser breadth, which *in any case* can only contain half the reality, as determined by the organization of the cognizing being. If one does not lose oneself in *abstractions*, one will realize that for a knowledge of human nature it is a relevant fact that in physics one has to *infer* the existence of elements in the perceptual field for which no sense organ is tuned as it is for colour or sound. Man's being, quite concretely, is determined not only by what his organization presents to him as immediate percept, but also by the fact that from this immediate perception other things are *excluded*. Just as it is necessary for life that in addition to the conscious waking state there should be an unconscious sleeping state, so for man's experience of himself it is necessary that in addition to the sphere of his sense perception there should be another sphere—in fact a far larger one—of elements not perceptible to the senses but belonging to the same field from which the sense percepts come. All this was already implied in the original presentation of this work. The author adds these extensions to the argument because he has found by experience that many a reader has not read accurately enough.

It is to be remembered, too, that the idea of *percept* developed in this book is not to be confused with the idea of external sense percept which is but a special instance of it. The reader will gather from what has gone before, but even more from what will follow, that "percept" is here taken to be everything that approaches man through the senses *or through the spirit*, before it has been grasped by the actively elaborated concept. "Senses", as we ordinarily understand the term, are not necessary in order to have percepts in soul- or spirit-experience. It might be said that this extension of our ordinary usage is not permissible. But such extension is *absolutely necessary* if we are not to be prevented by the current sense of a word from enlarging our knowledge in certain fields. Anyone who uses "perception" to mean *only* "sense perception" will never arrive at a concept fit for the purposes of knowledge—even knowledge of this same sense perception. One *must* sometimes enlarge a concept in order that it may get its appropriate meaning in a narrower field. Sometimes one must also add to the original content of a concept in order that the original concept may be justified or, perhaps, readjusted. Thus we find it said here in this book (page 84): "The mental picture is an individualized concept." It has been objected that this is an unusual use of words. But this use is necessary if we are to find out what a mental picture really is. How can we expect any progress in knowledge if everyone who finds himself compelled to readjust concepts is to be met by the objection, "This is an unusual use of words"?

THE REALITY OF FREEDOM

CHAPTER EIGHT

The Factors of Life

LET us recapitulate what we have achieved in the previous chapters. The world faces man as a multiplicity, as a mass of separate details. One of these separate things, one entity among others, is man himself. This aspect of the world we simply call the *given*, and inasmuch as we do not evolve it by conscious activity, but just find it, we call it *percept*. Within this world of percepts we perceive ourselves. This percept of self would remain merely one among many other percepts, if something did not arise from the midst of this percept of self which proves capable of connecting all percepts with one another and, therefore, the sum of all other percepts with the percept of our own self. This something which emerges is no longer merely percept; neither is it, like percepts, simply given. It is produced by our activity. To begin with, it appears to be bound up with what we perceive as our own self. In its inner significance, however, it transcends the self. To the separate percepts it adds ideally determined elements, which, however, are related to one another, and are rooted in a totality. What is obtained by perception of self is ideally determined by this something in the same way as are all other percepts, and is placed as subject, or "I", over against the objects. *This something is thinking*, and the ideally determined elements are the concepts and ideas. Thinking, therefore, first reveals itself in the percept of the self. But it is not merely subjective, for the self characterizes itself as subject only with the help of thinking.

This relationship in thought of the self to itself is what, in life, determines our personality. Through it we lead a purely ideal existence. Through it we feel ourselves to be thinking beings. This determination of our life would remain a purely conceptual (logical) one, if no other determinations of our self were added to it. We should then be creatures whose life was expended in establishing purely ideal relationships between percepts among themselves and between them and ourselves. If we call the establishment of such a thought connection an "act of cognition", and the resulting condition of ourself "knowledge", then, assuming the above supposition to be true, we should have to consider ourselves as beings who merely cognize or know.

The supposition, however, does not meet the case. We relate percepts to ourselves not merely ideally, through concepts, but also, as we have already seen, through feeling. Therefore we are not beings with a merely conceptual content to our life. In fact the naïve realist holds that the personality lives more genuinely in the life of feeling than in the purely ideal element of knowledge. From his point of view he is quite right when he describes the matter in this way. To begin with, feeling is exactly the same, on the subjective side, as the percept is on the objective side. From the basic principle of naïve realism—that everything that can be perceived is real—it follows that feeling must be the guarantee of the reality of one's own personality. Monism, however, as here understood, must grant the same addition to feeling that it considers necessary for percepts, if these are to stand before us as full reality. Thus, for monism, feeling is an incomplete reality, which, in the form in which it first appears to us, does not yet contain its second factor, the concept or idea. This is why, in actual life, feelings, like percepts, appear *prior* to knowledge. At first, we have merely a feeling of existence; and it is only in the course of our gradual development that we attain to the point at which the concept of self emerges from within the dim feeling of our own existence. However, what *for us* appears only later, is from the first indissolubly bound up with our feeling. This is why the naïve man comes to believe that in feeling he is presented with existence directly, in knowledge only indirectly. The cultivation of the life of feeling, therefore, appears to him more important than anything else. He will only believe that he has grasped the pattern of the universe when he has received it into his feeling. He attempts to make feeling, rather than knowing, the instrument of knowledge. Since a feeling is something entirely individual, something equivalent to a percept, the philosopher of feeling is making a universal principle out of something that has significance only within his own personality. He attempts to permeate the whole world with his own self. What the monist, in the sense we have described, strives to grasp through concepts, the philosopher of feeling tries to attain through feelings, and he regards this kind of connection with the objects as the more direct.

The tendency just described, the philosophy of feeling, is often called *mysticism*. The error in a mystical outlook based upon mere feeling is that it wants *to experience directly* what it ought to gain through *knowledge*; that it wants to raise feeling, which is individual, into a universal principle.

Feeling is a purely individual affair; it is the relation of the external world to ourself as subject, in so far as this relation finds expression in a merely subjective experience.

There is yet another expression of human personality. The I, through its thinking, shares the life of the world in general. In this manner, in a purely ideal way (that is, conceptually), it relates the percepts to itself, and itself to the percepts. In feeling, it has direct experience of a relation of the objects to itself as subject. In the *will*, the case is reversed. In willing, we are concerned once more with a percept, namely, that of the individual relation of our self to what is objective. Whatever there is in willing that is not a purely ideal factor, is just as much mere object of perception as is any object in the external world.

Nevertheless, the naïve realist believes here again that he has before him something far more real than can be attained by thinking. He sees in the will an element in which he is *directly* aware of an occurrence, a causation, in contrast with thinking which only grasps the event afterwards in conceptual form. According to such a view, what the I achieves through its will is a process which is experienced directly. The adherent of this philosophy believes that in the will he has really got hold of the machinery of the world by one corner. Whereas he can follow other occurrences only from the outside by means of perception, he is confident that in his will he experiences a real process quite directly. The mode of existence in which the will appears within the self becomes for him a concrete principle of reality. His own will appears to him as a special case of the general world process; hence the latter appears as universal will. The will becomes the principle of the universe just as, in mysticism, feeling becomes the principle of knowledge. This kind of theory is called the *philosophy of will* (thelism). It makes something that can be experienced only individually into a constituent factor of the world.

The philosophy of will can as little be called scientific as can the mysticism based on feeling. For both assert that the conceptual understanding of the world is inadequate. Both demand a principle of existence which is real, in addition to a principle which is ideal. To a certain extent this is justified. But since perceiving is our only means of apprehending these so-called real principles, the assertion of both the mysticism of feeling and the philosophy of will comes to the same thing as saying that we have two sources of knowledge, thinking and perceiving, the latter presenting itself as an individual experience in feeling and will. Since the results that flow from the one source, the experiences, cannot on this view be taken up directly into those that flow from the other source, thinking, the two modes of knowledge, perceiving and thinking, remain side by side without any higher form of mediation between them. Besides the ideal principle which is accessible to knowledge, there is said to be a real principle which cannot be apprehended by thinking but can yet be experienced. In other words, the mysticism of feeling and the philosophy of will are both forms of naïve realism, because they subscribe to the doctrine that what is directly perceived is real. Compared with naïve realism in its primitive form, they are guilty of the yet further inconsistency of accepting one particular form of perceiving (feeling or will, respectively) as the one and only means of knowing reality, whereas they can only do this at all if they hold in general to the fundamental principle that what is perceived is real. But in that case they ought to attach equal value, for the purposes of knowledge, also to external perception.

The philosophy of will turns into metaphysical realism when it places the element of will even into those spheres of existence where it cannot be experienced directly, as it can in the individual subject. It assumes, outside the subject, a hypothetical principle for whose real existence the sole criterion is subjective experience. As a form of metaphysical realism, the philosophy of will is subject to the criticism made in the preceding chapter, in that it has to get over the contradictory stage inherent in every form of metaphysical realism, and must acknowledge that the will is a universal world process only in so far as it is ideally related to the rest of the world.

Author's addition, 1918

The difficulty of grasping the essential nature of thinking by observation lies in this, that it has all too easily eluded the introspecting soul by the time the soul tries to bring it into the focus of attention. Nothing then remains to be inspected but the lifeless abstraction, the corpse of the living thinking. If we look only at this abstraction, we may easily find ourselves compelled to enter into the mysticism of feeling or perhaps the metaphysics of will, which by contrast appear so "full of life". We should then find it strange that anyone should expect to grasp the essence of reality in "mere thoughts". But if we once succeed in really finding *life in thinking*, we shall know that swimming in mere feelings, or being intuitively aware of the will element, cannot even be compared with the inner wealth and the self-sustaining yet ever moving *experience* of this life of thinking, let alone be ranked above it. It is owing precisely to this wealth, to this inward abundance of experience, that the counter-image of thinking which presents itself to our ordinary attitude of soul should appear lifeless and abstract. No other activity of the human soul is so easily misunderstood as thinking. Will and feeling still fill the soul with warmth even when we live through the original event again in retrospect. Thinking all too readily leaves us cold in recollection; it is as if the life of the soul had dried out. Yet this is really nothing but the strongly marked shadow of its real nature—warm, luminous, and penetrating deeply into the phenomena of the world. This penetration is brought about by a power flowing through the activity of thinking itself—the power of love in its spiritual form. There are no grounds here for the objection that to discern love in the activity of thinking is to project into thinking a feeling, namely, love. For in truth this objection is but a confirmation of what we have been saying. If we turn towards thinking *in its essence*, we find in it both feeling and will, and these in the depths of their reality; if we turn away from thinking towards "mere" feeling and will, we lose from these their true reality. If we are ready to experience thinking *intuitively*, we can also do justice to the experience of feeling and of will; but the mysticism of feeling and the metaphysics of will are not able to do justice to the penetration of reality by intuitive thinking—they conclude all too readily that they themselves are rooted in reality, but that the intuitive thinker, devoid of feeling and a stranger to reality, forms out of "abstract thoughts" a shadowy, chilly picture of the world.

CHAPTER NINE

The Idea of Freedom

FOR our cognition, the concept of the tree is conditioned by the percept of the tree. When faced with a particular percept, I can select only one particular concept from the general system of concepts. The connection of concept and percept is determined by thinking, indirectly and objectively, at the level of the percept. This connection of the percept with its concept is recognized *after* the act of perceiving; but that they do belong together lies in the very nature of things.

The process looks different when we examine *knowledge*, or rather the relation of man to the world which arises within knowledge. In the preceding chapters the attempt has been made to show that an unprejudiced observation of this relationship is able to throw light on its nature. A proper understanding of this observation leads to the insight that thinking can be *directly* discerned as a self-contained entity. Those who find it necessary for the explanation of thinking as such to invoke something else, such as physical brain processes or unconscious spiritual processes lying behind the conscious thinking which they observe, fail to recognize what an unprejudiced observation of thinking yields. When we observe our thinking, we live during this observation directly within a self-supporting, spiritual web of being. Indeed, we can even say that if we would grasp the essential nature of spirit in the form in which it presents itself *most immediately* to man, we need only look at the self-sustaining activity of thinking.

When we are contemplating thinking itself, two things coincide which otherwise *must* always appear apart, namely, concept and percept. If we fail to see this, we shall be unable to regard the concepts which we have elaborated with respect to percepts as anything but shadowy copies of these percepts, and we shall take the percepts as presenting to us the true reality. We shall, further, build up for ourselves a metaphysical world after the pattern of the perceived world; we shall call this a world of atoms, a world of will, a world of unconscious spirit, or whatever, each according to his own kind of mental imagery. And we shall fail to notice that all the time we have been doing nothing but building up a metaphysical world hypothetically, after the pattern of *our own* world of percepts. But if we recognize what is present in thinking, we shall realize that in the percept we have only one part of the reality and that the other part which belongs to it, and which first allows the full reality to appear, is *experienced* by us in the permeation of the percept by thinking. We shall see in this element that appears in our consciousness as thinking, not a shadowy copy of some reality, but a self-sustaining spiritual essence. And of this we shall be able to say that it is brought into consciousness for us through *intuition*. Intuition is the conscious experience —in pure spirit—of a purely spiritual content. Only through an intuition can the essence of thinking be grasped.

Only if, by means of unprejudiced observation, one has wrestled through to the recognition of this truth of the intuitive essence of thinking will one succeed in clearing the way for an insight into the psycho-physical organization of man. One will see that this organization can have no effect on the *essential nature* of thinking. At first sight this *seems* to be contradicted by patently obvious facts. For ordinary experience, human thinking makes its appearance only in connection with, and by means of, this organization. This form of its appearance comes so much to the fore that its real significance cannot be grasped unless we recognize that in the essence of thinking this organization plays no part whatever. Once we appreciate this, we can no longer fail to notice what a peculiar kind of relationship there is between the human organization and the thinking itself. For this organization contributes nothing to the essential nature of thinking, but recedes whenever the activity of thinking makes its appearance; it suspends its own activity, it yields ground; and on the ground thus left empty, the thinking appears. The essence which is active in thinking has a two-fold function: first, it represses the activity of the human organization; secondly, it steps into its place. For even the former, the repression of the physical organization, is a consequence of the activity of thinking, and more particularly of that part of this activity which prepares the *manifestation* of thinking. From this one can see in what sense thinking finds its counterpart in the physical organization. When we see this, we can no longer misjudge the significance of this counterpart of the activity of thinking. When we walk over soft ground, our feet leave impressions in the soil. We shall not be tempted to say that these footprints have been formed from below by the forces of the ground. We shall not attribute to *these* forces any share in the production of the footprints. Just as little, if we observe the essential nature of thinking without prejudice, shall we attribute any share in that nature to the traces in the physical organism which arise through the fact that the thinking prepares its manifestation by means of the body.*

* The way in which the above view has influenced psychology, physiology, etc., in various directions, has been set forth by the author in works published after this book. Here he is concerned

An important question, however, emerges here. If the human organization has no part in the *essential nature* of thinking, what is the significance of this organization within the whole nature of man? Now, what happens in this organization through the thinking has indeed nothing to do with the essence of thinking, but it has a great deal to do with the arising of the ego-consciousness out of this thinking. Thinking, in its own essential nature, certainly contains the real I or ego, but it does not contain the ego-consciousness. To see this we have but to observe thinking with an open mind. The "I" is to be found within the thinking; the "ego-consciousness" arises through the traces which the activity of thinking engraves upon our general consciousness, in the sense explained above. (The ego-consciousness thus arises through the bodily organization. However, this must not be taken to imply that the ego-consciousness, once it has arisen, remains dependent on the bodily organization. Once arisen, it is taken up into thinking and shares henceforth in thinking's spiritual being.)

The "ego-consciousness" is built upon the human organization. Out of the latter flow our acts of will. Following the lines of the preceding argument, we can gain insight into the connections between thinking, conscious I, and act of will, only by observing first how an act of will issues from the human organization.*

In any particular act of will we must take into account the motive and the driving force. The motive is a factor with the character of a concept or a mental picture; the driving force is the will-factor belonging to the human organization

---

only with characterizing the results of an unbiased observation of thinking itself.

* The passage from the beginning of the chapter down to this point was added or rewritten for the 1918 edition.

and directly conditioned by it. The conceptual factor, or motive, is the momentary determining factor of the will; the driving force is the permanent determining factor of the individual. A motive for the will may be a pure concept, or else a concept with a particular reference to a percept, that is, a mental picture. Both general concepts and individual ones (mental pictures) become motives of will by affecting the human individual and determining him to action in a particular direction. But one and the same concept, or one and the same mental picture, affects different individuals differently. They stimulate different men to different actions. An act of will is therefore not merely the outcome of the concept or the mental picture but also of the individual make-up of the person. Here we may well follow the example of Eduard von Hartmann and call this individual make-up the characterological disposition. The manner in which concept and mental picture affects the characterological disposition of a man gives to his life a definite moral or ethical stamp.

The characterological disposition is formed by the more or less permanent content of our subjective life, that is, by the content of our mental pictures and feelings. Whether a mental picture which enters my mind at this moment stimulates me to an act of will or not, depends on how it relates itself to the content of all my other mental pictures and also to my idiosyncrasies of feeling. But after all, the general content of my mental pictures is itself conditioned by the sum total of those concepts which have, in the course of my individual life, come into contact with percepts, that is, have become mental pictures. This sum, again, depends on my greater or lesser capacity for intuition and on the range of my observations, that is, on the subjective and objective factors of experience, on my inner nature and situation in life. My characterological disposition is determined especially by my life of feeling. Whether I shall make a particular mental picture or concept into a motive of action or not, will depend on whether it gives me joy or pain.

These are the elements which we have to consider in an act of will. The immediately present mental picture or concept, which becomes the motive, determines the aim or the purpose of my will; my characterological disposition determines me to direct my activity towards this aim. The mental picture of taking a walk in the next half-hour determines the aim of my action. But this mental picture is raised to the level of a motive for my will only if it meets with a suitable characterological disposition, that is, if during my past life I have formed the mental pictures of the sense and purpose of taking a walk, of the value of health, and further, if the mental picture of taking a walk is accompanied in me by a feeling of pleasure.

We must therefore distinguish (1) the possible subjective dispositions which are capable of turning certain mental pictures and concepts into motives, and (2) the possible mental pictures and concepts which are in a position to influence my characterological disposition so that an act of will results. For our moral life the former represent the *driving force*, and the latter, its *aims*.

The driving force in the moral life can be discovered by finding out the elements of which individual life is composed.

The first level of individual life is that of *perceiving*, more particularly perceiving through the senses. This is the region of our individual life in which perceiving translates itself directly into willing, without the intervention of either a feeling or a concept. The driving force here involved is simply called *instinct*. The satisfaction of our lower, purely animal needs (hunger, sexual intercourse, etc.) comes about

THE IDEA OF FREEDOM

in this way. The main characteristic of instinctive life is the immediacy with which the single percept releases the act of will. This kind of determination of the will, which belongs originally only to the life of the lower senses, may however become extended also to the percepts of the higher senses. We may react to the percept of a certain event in the external world without reflecting on what we do, without any special feeling connecting itself with the percept, as in fact happens in our conventional social behaviour. The driving force of such action is called *tact* or *moral good taste*. The more often such immediate reactions to a percept occur, the more the person concerned will prove himself able to act purely under the guidance of tact; that is, *tact* becomes his characterological disposition.

The second level of human life is *feeling*. Definite feelings accompany the percepts of the external world. These feelings may become the driving force of an action. When I see a starving man, my pity for him may become the driving force of my action. Such feelings, for example, are shame, pride, sense of honour, humility, remorse, pity, revenge, gratitude, piety, loyalty, love, and duty.*

The third level of life amounts to *thinking and forming mental pictures*. A mental picture or a concept may become the motive of an action through mere reflection. Mental pictures become motives because, in the course of life, we regularly connect certain aims of our will with percepts which recur again and again in more or less modified form. Hence with people not wholly devoid of experience it happens that the occurrence of certain percepts is always accompanied by

* A complete catalogue of the principles of morality (from the point of view of metaphysical realism) may be found in Eduard von Hartmann's *Phaenomenologie des sittlichen Bewusstseins*.

the appearance in consciousness of mental pictures of actions that they themselves have carried out in a similar case or have seen others carry out. These mental pictures float before their minds as patterns which determine all subsequent decisions; they become parts of their characterological disposition. The driving force in the will, in this case, we can call *practical experience*. Practical experience merges gradually into purely tactful behaviour. This happens when definite typical pictures of actions have become so firmly connected in our minds with mental pictures of certain situations in life that, in any given instance, we skip over all deliberation based on experience and go straight from the percept to the act of will.

The highest level of individual life is that of conceptual thinking without regard to any definite perceptual content. We determine the content of a concept through pure intuition from out of the ideal sphere. Such a concept contains, at first, no reference to any definite percepts. If we enter upon an act of will under the influence of a concept which refers to a percept, that is, under the influence of a mental picture, then it is this percept which determines our action indirectly by way of the conceptual thinking. But if we act under the influence of intuitions, the driving force of our action is *pure thinking*. As it is the custom in philosophy to call the faculty of pure thinking "reason", we may well be justified in giving the name of *practical reason* to the moral driving force characteristic of this level of life. The clearest account of this driving force in the will has been given by Kreyenbühl.* In my opinion his article on this subject is one of the most important contributions to present-day philosophy, more especially to Ethics. Kreyenbühl calls the driving force we are here discussing, the *practical a priori*,

* *Philosophische Monatshefte*, Vol. xviii, No. 3.

that is, an impulse to action issuing directly from my intuition.

It is clear that such an impulse can no longer be counted in the strictest sense as belonging to the characterological disposition. For what is here effective as the driving force is no longer something merely individual in me, but the ideal and hence universal content of my intuition. As soon as I see the justification for taking this content as the basis and starting point of an action, I enter upon the act of will irrespective of whether I have had the concept beforehand or whether it only enters my consciousness immediately before the action, that is, irrespective of whether it was already present as a disposition in me or not.

Since a real act of will results only when a momentary impulse to action, in the form of a concept or mental picture, acts on the characterological disposition, such an impulse then becomes the motive of the will.

The motives of moral conduct are mental pictures and concepts. There are Moral Philosophers who see a motive for moral behaviour also in the feelings; they assert, for instance, that the aim of moral action is to promote the greatest possible quantity of pleasure for the acting individual. Pleasure itself, however, cannot become a motive; only an *imagined pleasure* can. The *mental picture* of a future feeling, but not the feeling itself, can act on my characterological disposition. For the feeling itself does not yet exist in the moment of action; it has first to be produced by the action.

The *mental picture* of one's own or another's welfare is, however, rightly regarded as a motive of the will. The principle of producing the greatest quantity of pleasure for oneself through one's action, that is, of attaining individual happiness, is called *egoism*. The attainment of this individual happiness is sought either by thinking ruthlessly only of one's own good and striving to attain it even at the cost of the happiness of other individuals (pure egoism), or by promoting the good of others, either because one anticipates a favourable influence on one's own person indirectly through the happiness of others, or because one fears to endanger one's own interest by injuring others (morality of prudence). The special content of the egoistical principles of morality will depend on the mental pictures which we form of what constitutes our own, or others', happiness. A man will determine the content of his egoistical striving in accordance with what he regards as the good things of life (luxury, hope of happiness, deliverance from various evils, and so on).

The purely conceptual content of an action is to be regarded as yet another kind of motive. This content refers not to the particular action only, as with the mental picture of one's own pleasures, but to the derivation of an action from a system of moral principles. These moral principles, in the form of abstract concepts, may regulate the individual's moral life without his worrying himself about the origin of the concepts. In that case, we simply feel that submitting to a moral concept in the form of a commandment overshadowing our actions, is a moral necessity. The establishment of this necessity we leave to those who demand moral subjection from us, that is, to the moral authority that we acknowledge (the head of the family, the state, social custom, the authority of the church, divine revelation). It is a special kind of these moral principles when the commandment is made known to us not through an external authority but through our own inner life (moral autonomy). In this case we hear the voice to which we have to submit ourselves, in our own souls. This voice expresses itself as *conscience*.

It is a moral advance when a man no longer simply accepts

the commands of an outer or inner authority as the motive of his action, but tries to understand the reason why a particular maxim of behaviour should act as a motive in him. This is the advance from morality based on authority to action out of moral insight. At this level of morality a man will try to find out the requirements of the moral life and will let his actions be determined by the knowledge of them. Such requirements are

(1) the greatest possible good of mankind purely for its own sake;

(2) the progress of civilization, or the moral *evolution* of mankind towards ever greater perfection;

(3) the realization of individual moral aims grasped by pure intuition.

The *greatest possible good of mankind* will naturally be understood in different ways by different people. This maxim refers not to any particular mental picture of this "good" but to the fact that everyone who acknowledges this principle strives to do whatever, in his opinion, most promotes the good of mankind.

The *progress of civilization*, for those to whom the blessings of civilization bring a feeling of pleasure, turns out to be a special case of the foregoing moral principle. Of course, they will have to take into the bargain the decline and destruction of a number of things that also contribute to the general good. It is also possible, however, that some people regard the progress of civilization as a moral necessity quite apart from the feeling of pleasure that it brings. For them, this becomes a special moral principle in addition to the previous one.

The principle of the progress of civilization, like that of the general good, is based on a mental picture, that is, on the way we relate the content of our moral ideas to particular experiences (percepts). The highest conceivable moral principle, however, is one that from the start contains no such reference to particular experiences, but springs from the source of pure intuition and only later seeks any reference to percepts, that is, to life. Here the decision as to what is to be willed proceeds from an authority very different from that of the foregoing cases. If a man holds to the principle of the general good, he will, in all his actions, first ask what his ideals will contribute to this general good. If a man upholds the principle of the progress of civilization, he will act similarly. But there is a still higher way which does not start from one and the same particular moral aim in each case, but sees a certain value in all moral principles and always asks whether in the given case this or that principle is the more important. It may happen that in some circumstances a man considers the right aim to be the progress of civilization, in others the promotion of the general good, and in yet another the promotion of his own welfare, and in each case makes that the motive of his action. But if no other ground for decision claims more than second place, then conceptual intuition itself comes first and foremost into consideration. All other motives now give way, and the idea behind an action alone becomes its motive.

Among the levels of characterological disposition, we have singled out as the highest the one that works as *pure thinking* or *practical reason*. Among the motives, we have just singled out *conceptual intuition* as the highest. On closer inspection it will at once be seen that at this level of morality *driving force* and *motive* coincide; that is, neither a predetermined characterological disposition nor the external authority of an accepted moral principle influences our conduct. The action is therefore neither a stereotyped one which merely follows certain rules, nor is it one which we automatically perform in response to an external impulse, but it is an action determined purely and simply by its own ideal content.

Such an action presupposes the capacity for moral intuitions. Whoever lacks the capacity to experience for himself the particular moral principle for each single situation, will never achieve truly individual willing.

Kant's principle of morality—Act so that the basis of your action may be valid for all men—is the exact opposite of ours. His principle means death to all individual impulses of action. For me, the standard can never be the way *all* men would act, but rather what, for me, is to be done in each individual case.

A superficial judgment might raise the following objection to these arguments: How can an action be individually made to fit the special case and the special situation, and yet at the same time be determined by intuition in a purely ideal way? This objection rests upon a confusion of the moral motive with the perceptible content of an action. The latter *may* be a motive, and actually *is* one in the case of the progress of civilization, or when we act from egoism, and so forth, but in an action based on pure moral intuition it is *not* the motive. Of course, my "I" takes notice of these perceptual contents, but it does not allow itself to be *determined* by them. The content is used only to construct a *cognitive concept*, but the corresponding *moral concept* is not derived by the "I" from the object. The cognitive concept of a given situation facing me is at the same time a moral concept only if I take the standpoint of a particular moral principle. If I were to base my conduct only on the general principle of the development of civilization, then my way through life would be tied down to a fixed route. From every occurrence which I perceive and which concerns me, there springs at the same time a moral duty: namely, to do my little bit towards seeing that this occurrence is made to serve the development of civilization. In addition to the concept which reveals to me the connections of events or objects according to the laws of nature, there is also a moral label attached to them which for me, as a moral person, gives ethical directions as to how I have to conduct myself. Such a moral label is justified on its own ground; at a higher level it coincides with the idea which reveals itself to me when I am faced with the concrete instance.

Men vary greatly in their capacity for intuition. In one, ideas just bubble up; another acquires them with much labour. The situations in which men live and which provide the scenes of their actions are no less varied. The conduct of a man will therefore depend on the manner in which his faculty of intuition works in a given situation. The sum of ideas which are effective in us, the concrete content of our intuitions, constitutes what is individual in each of us, notwithstanding the universality of the world of ideas. In so far as this intuitive content applies to action, it constitutes the moral content of the individual. To let this content express itself in life is both the highest moral driving force and the highest motive a man can have, who sees that in this content all other moral principles are in the end united. We may call this point of view *ethical individualism.*

The decisive factor of an intuitively determined action in any concrete instance is the discovery of the corresponding purely individual intuition. At this level of morality one can only speak of general concepts of morality (standards, laws) in so far as these result from the generalization of the individual impulses. General standards always presuppose concrete facts from which they can be derived. But the facts have first to be *created* by human action.

If we seek out the rules (conceptual principles) underlying

the actions of individuals, peoples, and epochs, we obtain a system of ethics which is not so much a science of moral laws as a natural history of morality. It is only the laws obtained in this way that are related to human action as the laws of nature are related to a particular phenomenon. These laws, however, are by no means identical with the impulses on which we base our actions. If we want to understand how a man's action arises from his *moral* will, we must first study the relation of this will to the action. Above all, we must keep our eye on those actions in which this relation is the determining factor. If I, or someone else, reflect upon such an action afterwards, we can discover what moral principles come into question with regard to it. While I am performing the action I am influenced by a moral maxim in so far as it can live in me intuitively; it is bound up with my *love* for the objective that I want to realize through my action. I ask no man and no rule, "Shall I perform this action?"—but carry it out as soon as I have grasped the idea of it. This alone makes it *my* action. If a man acts only because he accepts certain moral standards, his action is the outcome of the principles which compose his moral code. He merely carries out orders. He is a superior automaton. Inject some stimulus to action into his mind, and at once the clockwork of his moral principles will set itself in motion and run its prescribed course, so as to result in an action which is Christian, or humane, or seemingly unselfish, or calculated to promote the progress of civilization. Only when I follow my love for my objective is it I myself who act. I act, at this level of morality, not because I acknowledge a lord over me, or an external authority, or a so-called inner voice; I acknowledge no external principle for my action, because I have found in myself the ground for my action, namely, my love of the action. I do not work out mentally whether my action is good

135

or bad; I carry it out because I *love* it. My action will be "good" if my intuition, steeped in love, finds its right place within the intuitively experienceable world continuum; it will be "bad" if this is not the case. Again, I do not ask myself, "How would another man act in my position?"—but I act as I, this particular individuality, find I have occasion to do. No general usage, no common custom, no maxim applying to all men, no moral standard is my immediate guide, but my love for the deed. I feel no compulsion, neither the compulsion of nature which guides me by my instincts, nor the compulsion of the moral commandments, but I want simply to carry out what lies within me.

Those who defend general moral standards might reply to these arguments that if everyone strives to live his own life and do what he pleases, there can be no distinction between a good deed and a crime; every corrupt impulse that lies within me has as good a claim to express itself as has the intention of serving the general good. What determines me as a moral being cannot be the mere fact of my having conceived the idea of an action, but whether I judge it to be good or *evil*. Only in the former case should I carry it out.

My reply to this very obvious objection, which is nevertheless based on a misapprehension of my argument, is this: If we want to understand the nature of the human will, we must distinguish between the path which leads this will to a certain degree of development and the unique character which the will assumes as it approaches this goal. On the path towards this goal the standards play their rightful part. The goal consists of the realization of moral aims grasped by pure intuition. Man attains such aims to the extent that he is able to raise himself at all to the intuitive world of ideas. In any particular act of will such moral aims will generally have other elements mixed in with them, either as driving force or as motive. Nevertheless intuition may still be wholly or partly the determining factor in the human will. What one *should* do, that one does; one provides the stage upon which obligation becomes deed; one's own action is what one brings forth from oneself. Here the impulse can only be wholly individual. And, in truth, only an act of will that springs from intuition can be an individual one. To regard evil, the deed of a criminal, as an expression of the human individuality in the same sense as one regards the embodiment of pure intuition is only possible if blind instincts are reckoned as part of the human individuality. But the blind instinct that drives a man to crime does not spring from intuition, and does not belong to what is individual in him, but rather to what is most general in him, to what is equally present in all individuals and out of which a man works his way by means of what is individual in him. What is individual in me is not my organism with its instincts and its feelings but rather the unified world of ideas which lights up within this organism. My instincts, urges and passions establish no more than that I belong to the general species *man*; it is the fact that something of the idea world comes to expression in a particular way within these urges, passions and feelings that establishes my individuality. Through my instincts and cravings, I am the sort of man of whom there are twelve to the dozen; through the particular form of the idea by means of which I designate myself within the dozen as "I", I am an individual. Only a being other than myself could distinguish me from others by the difference in my animal nature; through my thinking, that is, by actively grasping what expresses itself in my organism as idea, I distinguish myself from others. Therefore one cannot say of the action of a criminal that it proceeds from the idea within him. Indeed, the characteristic feature of criminal actions is precisely that they spring from the non-ideal elements in man.

An action is felt to be free in so far as the reasons for it spring from the ideal part of my individual being; every other part of an action, irrespective of whether it is carried out under the compulsion of nature or under the obligation of a moral standard, is felt to be *unfree*.

Man is free in so far as he is able to obey himself in every moment of his life. A moral deed is *my* deed only if it can be called a free one in this sense. We have here considered what conditions are required for an intentional action to be felt as a free one; how this purely ethically understood idea of freedom comes to realization in the being of man will be shown in what follows.

Acting out of freedom does not exclude the moral laws; it includes them, but shows itself to be on a higher level than those actions which are merely dictated by such laws. Why should my action be of less service to the public good when I have done it out of love than when I have done it *only* because I consider serving the public good to be my duty? The mere concept of duty excludes *freedom* because it does not acknowledge the individual element but demands that this be subject to a general standard. Freedom of action is conceivable only from the standpoint of ethical individualism.

But how is a social life possible for man if each one is only striving to assert his own individuality? This objection is characteristic of a false understanding of moralism. Such a moralist believes that a social community is possible only if all men are united by a communally fixed moral order. What this kind of moralist does not understand is just the unity of the world of ideas. He does not see that the world of ideas working in *me* is no other than the one working in my fellow man. Admittedly, this unity is but an outcome of practical experience. But in fact it *cannot* be anything else. For if it could be known in any other way than by observation, then in its own sphere universal standards rather than individual experience would be the rule. Individuality is possible only if every individual being knows of others through individual observation alone. I differ from my fellow man, not at all because we are living in two entirely different spiritual worlds, but because from the world of ideas common to us both we receive different intuitions. He wants to live out *his* intuitions, I *mine*. If we both really conceive out of the idea, and do not obey any external impulses (physical or spiritual), then we cannot but meet one another in like striving, in common intent. A moral misunderstanding, a clash, is impossible between men who are morally *free*. Only the morally unfree who follow their natural instincts or the accepted commands of duty come into conflict with their neighbours if these do not obey the same instincts and the same commands as themselves. To *live* in love towards our actions, and to *let live* in the understanding of the other person's will, is the fundamental maxim of *free men*. They know no other *obligation* than what their will puts itself in unison with intuitively; how they will direct their *will* in a particular case, their faculty for ideas will decide.

Were the ability to get on with one another not a basic part of human nature, no external laws would be able to implant it in us. It is only because human individuals *are* one in spirit that they can live out their lives side by side. The free man lives in confidence that he and any other free man belong to one spiritual world, and that their intentions will harmonize. The free man does not demand agreement from his fellow man, but expects to find it because it is inherent in human nature. I am not here referring to the necessity for this or that external institution, but to the *disposition*, the *attitude of soul,* through which a man, aware of himself among his fellows, most clearly expresses the ideal of human dignity.

There are many who will say that the concept of the *free* man which I have here developed is a chimera nowhere to be found in practice; we have to do with actual human beings, from whom we can only hope for morality if they obey some moral law, that is, if they regard their moral task as a duty and do not freely follow their inclinations and loves. I do not doubt this at all. Only a blind man could do so. But if this is to be the *final* conclusion, then away with all this hypocrisy about morality! Let us then simply say that human nature must be *driven* to its actions as long as it is not *free.* Whether his unfreedom is forced on him by physical means or by moral laws, whether man is unfree because he follows his unlimited sexual desire or because he is bound by the fetters of conventional morality, is quite immaterial from a certain point of view. Only let us not assert that such a man can rightly call his actions his *own,* seeing that he is driven to them by a force other than himself. But in the midst of all this framework of compulsion there arise men who establish themselves as *free spirits* in all the welter of customs, legal codes, religious observances, and so forth. They are *free* in so far as they obey only themselves, *unfree* in so far as they submit to control. Which of us can say that he is really free in all his actions? Yet in each of us there dwells a deeper being in which the free man finds expression.

Our life is made up of free and unfree actions. We cannot, however, think out the concept of man completely without coming upon the *free spirit* as the purest expression of human nature. Indeed, we are men in the true sense only in so far as we are free.

This is an ideal, many will say. Doubtless; but it is an

ideal which is a real element in us working its way to the surface of our nature. It is no ideal just thought up or dreamed, but one which has life, and which announces itself clearly even in the least perfect form of its existence. If man were merely a natural creature, there would be no such thing as the search for ideals, that is, for ideas which for the moment are not effective but whose realization is required. With the things of the outer world, the idea is determined by the percept; we have done our share when we have recognized the connection between idea and percept. But with the human being it is not so. The sum total of his existence is not fully determined without his own self; his true concept as a *moral* being (free spirit) is not objectively united from the start with the percept-picture "man" needing only to be confirmed by knowledge afterwards. Man must unite his concept with the percept of man by his own activity. Concept and percept coincide in this case only if man himself makes them coincide. This he can do only if he has found the concept of the free spirit, that is, if he has found the concept of his own self. In the objective world a dividing line is drawn by our organization between percept and concept; knowledge overcomes this division. In our subjective nature this division is no less present; man overcomes it in the course of his development by bringing the concept of himself to expression in his outward existence. Hence not only man's intellectual but also his moral life leads to his two-fold nature, perceiving (direct experience) and thinking. The intellectual life overcomes this two-fold nature by means of knowledge, the moral life overcomes it through the actual realization of the free spirit. Every existing thing has its inborn concept (the law of its being and doing), but in external objects this concept is indivisibly bound up with the percept, and separated from it only within our spiritual organization.

In man concept and percept are, at first, *actually* separated, to be just as *actually* united by him.

One might object: At every moment of a man's life there is a definite concept corresponding to our percept of him just as with everything else. I can form for myself the concept of a particular type of man, and I may even find such a man given to me as a percept; if I now add to this the concept of a free spirit, then I have two concepts for the same object.

Such an objection is one-sided. As object of perception I am subjected to continual change. As a child I was one thing, another as a youth, yet another as a man. Indeed, at every moment the percept-picture of myself is different from what it was the moment before. These changes may take place in such a way that it is always the same man (the type) who reveals himself in them, or that they represent the expression of a free spirit. To such changes my action, as object of perception, is subjected.

The perceptual object "man" has in it the possibility of transforming itself, just as the plant seed contains the possibility of becoming a complete plant. The plant transforms itself because of the objective law inherent in it; the human being remains in his incomplete state unless he takes hold of the material for transformation within him and transforms himself through his own power. Nature makes of man merely a natural being; society makes of him a law-abiding being; only *he himself* can make of himself a *free man*. Nature releases man from her fetters at a definite stage in his development; society carries this development a stage further; he alone can give himself the final polish.

The standpoint of free morality, then, does not declare the free spirit to be the only form in which a man can exist. It sees in the free spirit only the last stage of man's evolution. This is not to deny that conduct according to standards has its justification as one stage in evolution. Only we cannot acknowledge it as the absolute standpoint in morality. For the free spirit overcomes the standards in the sense that he does not just accept commandments as his motives but orders his action according to his own impulses (intuitions).

When Kant says of duty: "Duty! Thou exalted and mighty name, thou that dost comprise nothing lovable, nothing ingratiating, but demandest submission," thou that "settest up a law . . . before which all inclinations are silent, even though they secretly work against it,"* then out of the consciousness of the free spirit, man replies: "Freedom! Thou kindly and human name, thou that dost comprise all that is morally most lovable, all that my manhood most prizes, and that makest me the servant of nobody, thou that settest up no mere law, but awaitest what my moral love itself will recognize as law because in the face of every merely imposed law it feels itself unfree."

This is the contrast between a morality based on mere law and a morality based on inner freedom.

The philistine, who sees the embodiment of morality in an external code, may see in the free spirit even a dangerous person. But that is only because his view is narrowed down to a limited period of time. If he were able to look beyond this, he would at once find that the free spirit just as seldom needs to go beyond the laws of his state as does the philistine himself, and certainly never needs to place himself in real opposition to them. For the laws of the state, one and all, just like all other objective laws of morality, have had their origin in the intuitions of free spirits. There is no rule enforced by family authority that was not at one time intuitively grasped and laid down as such by an ancestor; similarly the conventional laws of morality are first of all

* *Critique of Practical Reason*, chapter iii.

established by definite men, and the laws of the state always originate in the head of a statesman. These leading spirits have set up laws over other men, and the only person who feels unfree is the one who forgets this origin and either turns these laws into extra-human commandments, objective moral concepts of duty independent of man, or else turns them into the commanding voice within himself which he supposes, in a falsely mystical way, to be compelling him. On the other hand, the person who does not overlook this origin, but seeks man within it, will count such laws as belonging to the same world of ideas from which he, too, draws his moral intuitions. If he believes he has better intuitions, he will try to put them into the place of the existing ones; if he finds the existing ones justified, he will act in accordance with them as if they were his own.

We must not coin the formula: Man exists only in order to realize a moral world order which is quite distinct from himself. Anyone who maintains that this is so, remains, in his knowledge of man, at the point where natural science stood when it believed that a bull has horns in order to butt. Scientists, happily, have thrown out the concept of purpose as a dead theory. Ethics finds it more difficult to get free of this concept. But just as horns do not exist *for the sake* of butting, but butting through the presence of horns, so man does not exist *for the sake* of morality, but morality through the presence of man. The free man acts morally because he has a moral idea; he does not act in order that morality may come into being. Human individuals, with the moral ideas belonging to their nature, are the prerequisites of a moral world order.

The human individual is the source of all morality and the centre of earthly life. State and society exist only because they have arisen as a necessary consequence of the life of individuals. That state and society should in turn react upon individual life is no more difficult to comprehend than that the butting which is the result of the presence of horns reacts in turn upon the further development of the horns of the bull, which would become stunted through prolonged disuse. Similarly, the individual would become stunted if he led an isolated existence outside human society. Indeed, this is just why the social order arises, so that it may in turn react favourably upon the individual.

CHAPTER TEN

Freedom-Philosophy and Monism

THE naïve man, who acknowledges as real only what he can see with his eyes and grasp with his hands, requires for his moral life, also, a basis for action that shall be perceptible to the senses. He requires someone or something to impart the basis for his action to him in a way that his senses can understand. He is ready to allow this basis for action to be dictated to him as commandments by any man whom he considers wiser or more powerful than himself, or whom he acknowledges for some other reason to be a power over him. In this way there arise, as moral principles, the authority of family, state, society, church and God, as previously described. A man who is very narrow minded still puts his faith in some one person; the more advanced man allows his moral conduct to be dictated by a majority (state, society). It is always on perceptible powers that he builds. The man who awakens at last to the conviction that basically these powers are human beings as weak as himself, seeks guidance from a higher power, from a Divine Being, whom he endows, however, with sense perceptible features. He conceives this Being as communicating to him the conceptual content of his moral life, again in a perceptible way—whether it be, for example, that God appears in the burning bush, or that He moves about among men in manifest human shape, and that their ears can hear Him telling them what to do and what not to do.

The highest stage of development of naïve realism in the sphere of morality is that where the moral commandment (moral idea) is separated from every being other than one-self and is thought of, hypothetically, as being an absolute power in one's own inner life. What man first took to be the external voice of God, he now takes as an independent power within him, and speaks of this inner voice in such a way as to identify it with conscience.

But in doing this he has already gone beyond the stage of naïve consciousness into the sphere where the moral laws have become independently existing standards. There they are no longer carried by real bearers, but have become metaphysical entities existing in their own right. They are analogous to the invisible "visible forces" of metaphysical realism, which does not seek reality through the part of it that man has in his thinking, but hypothetically adds it on to actual experience. These extra-human moral standards always occur as accompanying features of metaphysical realism. For metaphysical realism is bound to seek the origin of morality in the sphere of extra-human reality. Here there are several possibilities. If the hypothetically assumed entity is conceived as in itself unthinking, acting according to purely mechanical laws, as materialism would have it, then it must also produce out of itself, by purely mechanical necessity, the human individual with all his characteristic features. The consciousness of freedom can then be nothing more than an illusion. For though I con-sider myself the author of my action, it is the matter of which I am composed and the movements going on in it that are working in me. I believe myself free; but in fact all my actions are nothing but the result of the material pro-cesses which underlie my physical and mental organization. It is said that we have the feeling of freedom only because we do not know the motives compelling us.

We must emphasize that the feeling of freedom is due to the absence of external compelling motives. . . . Our action is necessitated as is our thinking.*

Another possibility is that a man may picture the extra-human Absolute that lies behind the world of appearances as a spiritual being. In this case he will also seek the impulse for his actions in a corresponding spiritual force. He will see the moral principles to be found in his own reason as the expression of this being itself, which has its own special intentions with regard to man. To this kind of dualist the moral laws appear to be dictated by the Absolute, and all that man has to do is to use his intelligence to find out the decisions of the absolute being and then carry them out. The moral world order appears to the dualist as the perceptible reflection of a higher order standing behind it. Earthly morality is the manifestation of the extra-human world order. It is not man that matters in this moral order, but the being itself, that is, the extra-human entity. Man *shall* do as this being *wills*. Eduard von Hartmann, who imagines this being itself as a Godhead whose very existence is a life of suffering, believes that this Divine Being has created the world in order thereby to gain release from His infinite suffering. Hence this philosopher regards the moral evolution of humanity as a process which is there for the redemption of God.

Only through the building up of a moral world order by intelligent self-conscious individuals can the world process be led towards its goal. . . . True existence is the incarnation of the Godhead; the world process is the Passion of the

* Ziehen, *Leitfaden der physiologischen Psychologie*, 1st edition, pp. 207 ff. For the way I have here spoken about "materialism", and the justification for doing so, see the *Addition* to this chapter, p. 154.

incarnated Godhead and at the same time the way of redemption for Him who was crucified in the flesh; *morality, however, is the collaboration in the shortening of this path of suffering and redemption.**

Here man does not act because he wants to, but he *shall* act, because it is God's will to be redeemed. Whereas the materialistic dualist makes man an automaton whose actions are only the result of a purely mechanical system, the spiritualistic dualist (that is, one who sees the Absolute, the Being-in-itself, as something spiritual in which man has no share in his conscious experience) makes him a slave to the will of the Absolute. As in materialism, so also in one-sided spiritualism, in fact in any kind of metaphysical realism inferring but not experiencing something extra-human as the true reality, freedom is out of the question.

Metaphysical as well as naïve realism, consistently followed out, must deny freedom for one and the same reason: they both see man as doing no more than putting into effect, or carrying out, principles forced upon him by necessity. Naïve realism destroys freedom by subjecting man to the authority of a perceptible being or of one conceived on the analogy of a perceptible being, or eventually to the authority of the abstract inner voice which it *interprets* as "conscience"; the metaphysician, who merely infers the extra-human reality, cannot acknowledge freedom because he sees man as being determined, mechanically or morally, by a "Being-in-itself".

Monism will have to recognize that naïve realism is partially justified because it recognizes the justification of the world of percepts. Whoever is incapable of producing moral ideas through intuition must accept them from others. In so far as a man receives his moral principles from without, he is in

* Hartmann, *Phaenomenologie des sittlichen Bewusstseins*, p. 871.

fact unfree. But monism attaches as much significance to the idea as to the percept. The idea, however, can come to manifestation in the human individual. In so far as man follows the impulses coming from this side, he feels himself to be free. But monism denies all justification to metaphysics, which merely draws inferences, and consequently also to the impulses of action which are derived from so-called "Beings-in-themselves". According to the monistic view, man may act unfreely—when he obeys some perceptible external compulsion; he can act freely, when he obeys none but himself. Monism cannot recognize any unconscious compulsion hidden behind percept and concept. If anyone asserts that the action of a fellow man is done *unfreely*, then he must identify the thing or the person or the institution within the perceptible world, that has caused the person to act; and if he bases his assertion upon causes of action lying *outside* the world that is real to the senses and the spirit, then monism can take no notice of it.

According to the monistic view, then, man's action is partly unfree, partly free. He finds himself to be *unfree* in the world of percepts, and he realizes within himself the *free* spirit.

The moral laws which the metaphysician who works by mere inference must regard as issuing from a higher power, are, for the adherent of monism, *thoughts of men*; for him the moral world order is neither the imprint of a purely mechanical natural order, nor that of an extra-human world order, but through and through the free creation of men. It is not the will of some being outside him in the world that man has to carry out, but his own; he puts into effect his own resolves and intentions, not those of another being. Monism does not see, behind man's actions, the purposes of a supreme directorate, foreign to him and determining him according to its will, but rather sees that men, in so far as they realize their intuitive ideas, pursue only their own *human* ends. Moreover, each individual pursues his own particular ends. For the world of ideas comes to expression, not in a community of men, but only in human individuals. What appears as the common goal of a whole group of people is only the result of the separate acts of will of its individual members, and in fact, usually of a few outstanding ones who, as their authorities, are followed by the others. Each one of us has it in him to be a *free spirit*, just as every rose bud has in it a rose.

Monism, then, in the sphere of true moral action, is a *freedom philosophy*. Since it is a philosophy of reality, it rejects the metaphysical, unreal restrictions of the free spirit as completely as it accepts the physical and historical (naïvely real) restrictions of the naïve man. Since it does not consider man as a finished product, disclosing his full nature in every moment of his life, it regards the dispute as to whether man as such *is free or not*, to be of no consequence. It sees in man a developing being, and asks whether, in the course of this development, the stage of the free spirit can be reached.

Monism knows that Nature does not send man forth from her arms ready made as a free spirit, but that she leads him up to a certain stage from which he continues to develop still as an unfree being until he comes to the point where he finds his own self.

Monism is quite clear that a being acting under physical or moral compulsion cannot be a truly moral being. It regards the phases of automatic behaviour (following natural urges and instincts) and of obedient behaviour (following moral standards) as necessary preparatory stages of morality, but it also sees that both these transitory stages can be overcome by the free spirit. Monism frees the truly moral world conception both from the mundane fetters of naïve moral maxims and from the transcendental moral maxims of the speculative metaphysician. Monism can no more eliminate the former from the world than it can eliminate percepts; it rejects the latter because it seeks all the principles for the elucidation of the world phenomena *within* that world, and none outside it.

Just as monism refuses even to think of principles of knowledge other than those that apply to men (see page 100), so it emphatically rejects even the thought of moral maxims other than those that apply to men. Human morality, like human knowledge, is conditioned by human nature. And just as beings of a different order will understand knowledge to mean something very different from what it means to us, so will other beings have a different morality from ours. Morality is for the monist a specifically human quality, and spiritual *freedom* the human way of being moral.

Author's additions, 1918

1. In forming a judgment about the argument of the two preceding chapters, a difficulty can arise in that one appears to be faced with a contradiction. On the one hand we have spoken of the experience of thinking, which is felt to have universal significance, equally valid for every human consciousness; on the other hand we have shown that the ideas which come to realization in the moral life, and are of the same kind as those elaborated in thinking, come to expression in each human consciousness in a quite individual way. If we cannot get beyond regarding this antithesis as a "contradiction", and if we do not see that in the *living recognition* of this *actually existing* antithesis a piece of man's essential nature reveals itself, then we shall be unable to see either the idea of knowledge or the idea of freedom in a true light. For those who think of their concepts as merely abstracted from the sense perceptible world and who do not allow intuition its rightful place, this thought, here claimed as a reality, must remain a "mere contradiction". If we really understand how ideas are intuitively *experienced* in their self-sustaining essence, it becomes clear that *in the act of knowing*, man, on the edge of the world of ideas, lives his way into something which is the same for all men, but that when, from this world of ideas, he derives the intuitions for his acts of will, he individualizes a part of this world by *the same activity* that he practices as a universal human one in the spiritual ideal process of knowing. What appears as a logical contradiction between the universal nature of cognitive ideas and the individual nature of moral ideas is the very thing that, when seen *in its reality*, becomes a living

concept. It is a characteristic feature of the essential nature of man that what can be intuitively grasped swings to and fro within man, like a living pendulum, between universally valid knowledge and the individual experience of it. For those who cannot see the one half of the swing in its reality, thinking remains only a subjective human activity; for those who cannot grasp the other half, man's activity in thinking will seem to lose all individual life. For the first kind of thinker, it is the act of knowing that is an unintelligible fact; for the second kind, it is the moral life. Both will put forward all sorts of imagined ways of explaining the one or the other, all equally unfounded, either because they entirely fail to grasp that thinking can be actually experienced, or because they misunderstand it as a merely abstracting activity.

*　*　*　*　*

2. On page 147 I have spoken of materialism. I am well aware that there are thinkers—such as Ziehen, mentioned above—who do not call themselves materialists at all, but who must nevertheless be described as such from the point of view put forward in this book. The point is not whether someone says that for him the world is not restricted to merely material existence and that therefore he is no materialist; but the point is whether he develops concepts which are applicable *only* to material existence. Anyone who says, "Our action is necessitated as is our thinking", has implied a concept which is applicable only to material processes, but not to action or to being; and if he were to think his concept through to the end, he could not help but think materialistically. He avoids doing this only by the same inconsistency that so often results from not thinking one's thoughts through to the end.

It is often said nowadays that the materialism of the

nineteenth century is outmoded in knowledgeable circles. But in fact this is not at all true. It is only that nowadays people so often fail to notice that they have no other ideas but those with which one can approach only material things. Thus recent materialism is veiled, whereas in the second half of the nineteenth century it showed itself openly. The veiled materialism of the present is no less intolerant of an outlook that grasps the world spiritually than was the self-confessed materialism of the last century. But it deceives many who think they have a right to reject a view of the world which takes spirit into account on the ground that the scientific view "has long ago abandoned materialism".

CHAPTER ELEVEN

World Purpose and Life Purpose
(The Ordering of Man's Destiny)

AMONG the manifold currents in the spiritual life of mankind, there is one to be followed up which can be described as the overcoming of the concept of purpose in spheres where it does not belong. *Purposefulness* is a special kind of sequence of phenomena. True purposefulness really exists only if, in contrast to the relationship of cause and effect where the earlier event determines the later, the reverse is the case and the later event influences the earlier one. To begin with, this happens only in the case of human actions. One performs an action of which one has *previously* made a mental picture, and one allows this mental picture to determine one's action. Thus the *later* (the deed) influences the *earlier* (the doer) with the help of the mental picture. For there to be a purposeful connection, this detour through the mental picture is absolutely necessary.

In a process which breaks down into cause and effect, we must distinguish percept from concept. The percept of the cause precedes the percept of the effect; cause and effect would simply remain side by side in our consciousness, if we were not able to connect them with one another through their corresponding concepts. The percept of the effect must always follow upon the percept of the cause. If the effect is to have a real influence upon the cause, it can do so only by means of the conceptual factor. For the perceptual factor of the effect simply does not exist prior to the perceptual factor of the cause. Anyone who declares that the blossom is the purpose of the root, that is, that the former influences the latter, can do so only with regard to that factor in the blossom which is established in it by his thinking. The perceptual factor of the blossom is not yet in existence at the time when the root originates.

For a purposeful connection to exist, it is not only necessary to have an ideal, law-determined connection between the later and the earlier, but the concept (law) of the effect must *really* influence the cause, that is, by means of a perceptible process. A perceptible influence of a concept upon something else, however, is to be observed only in human actions. Hence this is the only sphere in which the concept of purpose is applicable.

The naïve consciousness, which regards as real only what is perceptible, attempts—as we have repeatedly pointed out—to introduce perceptible elements where only ideal elements are to be found. In the perceptible course of events it looks for perceptible connections, or, failing to find them, it simply *invents* them. The concept of purpose, valid for subjective actions, is an element well suited for such invented connections. The naïve man knows how he brings an event about and from this he concludes that nature will do it in the same way. In the connections of nature which are purely ideal he finds not only invisible forces but also invisible real purposes. Man makes his tools according to his purposes; the naïve realist would have the Creator build organisms on the same formula. Only very gradually is this mistaken concept of purpose disappearing from the sciences. In philosophy, even today, it still does a good deal of mischief. Here people still ask after the extra-mundane purpose of the world, the extra-human ordering of man's destiny (and consequently also his purpose), and so on.

Monism rejects the concept of purpose in every sphere, with the sole exception of human action. It looks for laws of nature, but not for purposes of nature. *Purposes of nature* are arbitrary assumptions no less than are imperceptible forces (see page 97). But even purposes of life not set by man himself are unjustified assumptions from the standpoint of monism. Nothing is purposeful except what man has first made so, for purposefulness arises only through the realization of an idea. In a realistic sense, an idea can become effective only in man. Therefore human life can only have the purpose and the ordering of destiny that man gives it. To the question: What is man's task in life? there can be for monism but one answer: The task he sets himself. My mission in the world is not predetermined, but is at every moment the one I choose for myself. I do not set out upon my journey through life with fixed marching orders.

Ideas are realized purposefully only by human beings. Consequently it is not permissible to speak of the embodiment of ideas by history. All such phrases as "history is the evolution of mankind towards freedom," or ". . . the realization of the moral world order," and so on, are, from a monistic point of view, untenable.

The supporters of the concept of purpose believe that, by surrendering it, they would also have to surrender all order and uniformity in the world. Listen, for example, to Robert Hamerling:

As long as there are *instincts* in nature, it is folly to deny *purposes* therein.

Just as the formation of a limb of the human body is not determined and conditioned by an idea of this limb, floating in the air, but by its connection with the greater whole, the body to which the limb belongs, so the formation of every natural object, be it plant, animal or man, is not determined and conditioned by an idea of it floating in the air, but by the formative principle of the totality of nature which unfolds and organizes itself in a purposeful manner.*

And on page 191 of the same volume we read:

> The theory of purpose maintains only that, *in spite of* the thousand discomforts and distresses of this mortal life, there is a high degree of purpose and plan unmistakably present in the formations and developments of nature—a degree of plan and purposefulness, however, which is realized only within the limits of natural law, and which does not aim at a fool's paradise where life faces no death, growth no decay, with all their more or less unpleasant but quite unavoidable intermediary stages.
>
> When the opponents of the concept of purpose set a laboriously collected rubbish-heap of partial or complete, imaginary or real maladaptations against a whole world of miracles of purposefulness, such as nature exhibits in all her domains, then I consider this just as quaint . . .

What is here meant by purposefulness? The coherence of percepts to form a whole. But since underlying all percepts there are laws (ideas) which we discover through our thinking, it follows that the systematic coherence of the parts of a perceptual whole is simply the ideal coherence of the parts of an ideal whole contained in this perceptual whole. To say that an animal or a man is not determined by an *idea floating in the air* is a misleading way of putting it, and the point of view he is disparaging automatically loses its absurdity as soon as the expression is put right. An animal certainly is not determined by an idea floating in the air, but it definitely is determined by an idea inborn in it and constituting the law of its being. It is just because the idea is not external to the object, but works within it as its very essence, that we

* *Atomistik des Willens*, vol ii, p. 201.

cannot speak of purposefulness. It is just the person who denies that natural beings are determined from without (and it does not matter, in this context, whether it be by an idea floating in the air or existing *outside* the creature in the mind of a world creator) who must admit that such beings are not determined by purpose and plan from without, but by cause and law from within. I construct a machine purposefully if I connect its parts together in a way that is not given in nature. The purposefulness of the arrangement consists in just this, that I embody the working principle of the machine, as its idea, into the machine itself. The machine becomes thereby an object of perception with the idea corresponding to it. Natural objects are also entities of this kind. Whoever calls a thing purposeful simply because it is formed according to a law, may, if he wish, apply the same term to the objects of nature. But he must not confuse this kind of lawfulness with that of subjective human action. For *purpose* to exist, it is absolutely necessary that the effective cause shall be a concept, in fact the concept of the effect. But in nature we can nowhere point to concepts acting as causes; the concept invariably turns out to be nothing but the ideal link connecting cause and effect. Causes are present in nature only in the form of percepts.

Dualism may talk of world purposes and natural purposes. Wherever there is a systematic linking of cause and effect for our perception, the dualist may assume that we see only the carbon copy of a connection in which the absolute cosmic Being has realized its purposes. For monism, with the rejection of an absolute cosmic Being—never experienced but only hypothetically inferred—all ground for assuming purposes in the world and in nature also falls away.

Author's addition, 1918

No one who has followed the preceding argument with an open mind will be able to conclude that the author, in rejecting the concept of purpose for extra-human facts, takes the side of those thinkers who, by rejecting this concept, enable themselves to regard everything outside human action —and thence human action itself—as no more than a natural process. He should be protected from this by the fact that in this book the thinking process is presented as a purely spiritual one. If here the concept of purpose is rejected even for the *spiritual* world, lying outside human action, it is because something is revealed in that world which is *higher* than the kind of purpose realized in the human kingdom. And when we say that the thought of a purposeful destiny for the human race, modelled on human purposefulness, is erroneous, we mean that the individual gives himself purposes, and that the outcome of the working of mankind as a whole is compounded of these. This outcome is then something *higher* than its component parts, the purposes of men.

CHAPTER TWELVE

Moral Imagination
(*Darwinism and Morality*)

A *free spirit* acts according to his impulses, that is, according
to intuitions selected from the totality of his world of ideas by
thinking. For an *unfree spirit*, the reason why he singles out a
particular intuition from his world of ideas in order to make
it the basis of an action, lies in the world of percepts given
to him, that is, in his past experiences. He recalls, before
coming to a decision, what someone else has done or recommended as suitable in a comparable case, or what God has
commanded to be done in such a case, and so on, and he acts
accordingly. For a free spirit, these prior conditions are not
the only impulses to action. He makes a completely *first-hand*
decision. What others have done in such a case worries him as
little as what they have decreed. He has purely ideal reasons
which lead him to select from the sum of his concepts just
one in particular, and then to translate it into action. But his
action will belong to perceptible reality. What he achieves
will thus be identical with a quite definite content of perception. The concept will have to realize itself in a single
concrete occurrence. As a concept it will not be able to contain
this particular event. It will refer to the event only in the
same way as a concept is in general related to a percept, for
example, the concept of the lion to a particular lion. The link
between concept and percept is the *mental picture* (see page
84). For the unfree spirit, this link is given from the outset.
Motives are present in his consciousness from the outset in
the form of mental pictures. Whenever there is something he

wants to carry out, he does it as he has seen it done, or as he has been told to do it in the particular case. Hence authority works best through *examples*, that is, through providing quite definite particular actions for the consciousness of the unfree spirit. A Christian acts not so much according to the teaching as according to the *example* of the Saviour. Rules have less value for acting positively than for refraining from certain actions. Laws take on the form of general concepts only when they forbid actions, but not when they prescribe them. Laws concerning what he ought to do must be given to the unfree spirit in quite concrete form: Clean the street in front of your door! Pay your taxes, amounting to the sum here given, to the Tax Office at X! and so on. Conceptual form belongs to laws for inhibiting actions: Thou shalt *not* steal! Thou shalt *not* commit adultery! These laws, too, influence the unfree spirit only by means of a concrete mental picture, for example, that of the appropriate secular punishment, or the pangs of conscience, or eternal damnation, and so on.

Whenever the impulse for an action is present in a general conceptual form (for example, Thou shalt do good to thy fellow men! Thou shalt live so that thou best promotest thy welfare!) then for each particular case the concrete mental picture of the action (the relation of the concept to a content of perception) must first be found. For the *free spirit* who is impelled by no example, nor fear of punishment or the like, this translation of the concept into a mental picture is always necessary.

Man produces concrete mental pictures from the sum of his ideas chiefly by means of the imagination. Therefore what the free spirit needs in order to realize his ideas, in order to be effective, is *moral imagination*. This is the source of the free spirit's action. Therefore it is only men with moral imagination who are, strictly speaking, morally productive. Those who merely preach morality, that is, people who merely spin out moral rules without being able to condense them into concrete mental pictures, are morally unproductive. They are like those critics who can explain very intelligibly what a work of art ought to be like, but who are themselves incapable of even the slightest productive effort.

Moral imagination, in order to realize its mental picture, must set to work in a definite sphere of percepts. Human action does not create percepts, but transforms already existing percepts and gives them a new form. In order to be able to transform a definite object of perception, or a sum of such objects, in accordance with a moral mental picture, one must have grasped the principle at work within the percept picture, that is, the way it has hitherto worked, to which one wants to give a new form or a new direction. Further, it is necessary to discover the procedure by which it is possible to change the given principle into a new one. This part of effective moral activity depends on knowledge of the particular world of phenomena with which one is concerned. We shall, therefore, look for it in some branch of learning in general. Moral action, then, presupposes, in addition to the faculty of having moral ideas (moral intuition) and moral imagination, the ability to transform the world of percepts without violating the natural laws by which these are connected.* This ability is *moral technique*. It can be learnt in the same sense in which any kind of knowledge can be learnt. Generally speaking, men are better able to find

* Only a superficial critic will find in the use of the word "faculty" in this and other passages a relapse into the doctrine of faculties of the soul, found in the older psychology. The meaning of the word is clear when taken in connection with what is said on p. 73.

concepts for the existing world than to evolve productively, out of their imagination, the not-yet-existing actions of the future. Hence it is perfectly possible for men without moral imagination to receive such mental pictures from others, and to embody them skilfully into the actual world. Conversely, it may happen that men with moral imagination lack technical skill, and must make use of other men for the realization of their mental pictures.

In so far as knowledge of the objects within our sphere of action is necessary for acting morally, our action depends upon such knowledge. What we are concerned with here are *laws of nature*. We are dealing with natural science, not ethics.

Moral imagination and the faculty of having moral ideas can become objects of knowledge only *after* they have been produced by the individual. By then, however, they no longer regulate life, for they have already regulated it. They must now be regarded as effective causes, like all others (they are purposes only for the subject). We therefore deal with them as with a *natural history of moral ideas*.

Ethics as a science that sets standards, in addition to this, cannot exist.

Some people have wanted to maintain the standard-setting character of moral laws, at least in so far as they have understood ethics in the sense of dietetics, which deduces general rules from the organism's requirements in life as a basis for influencing the body in a particular way (e.g., Paulsen, in his *System der Ethik*). This comparison is false, because our moral life is not comparable with the life of the organism. The functioning of the organism occurs without any action on our part; we come upon its laws in the world ready-made and can therefore seek them and apply them when found. Moral laws, on the other hand, are first created by us. We cannot apply them until we have created them. The error arises through the fact that, as regards their content, moral laws are not newly created at every moment, but are inherited. Those that we have taken over from our ancestors appear to be given, like the natural laws of the organism. But a later generation will certainly not be justified in applying them as if they were dietetic rules. For they apply to individuals and not, as natural laws do, to specimens of a general type. Considered as an organism, I am such a generic specimen and I shall live in accordance with nature if I apply the natural laws of my general type to my particular case; as a moral being, I am an individual and have laws of my very own.*

This view appears to contradict the fundamental doctrine of modern natural science known as the *theory of evolution*. But it only *appears* to do so. Evolution is understood to mean the *real* development of the later out of the earlier in accordance with natural law. In the organic world, evolution is understood to mean that the later (more perfect) organic forms are real descendants of the earlier (imperfect) forms, and have developed from them in accordance with natural laws. The adherents of the theory of organic evolution ought really to picture to themselves that there was once a time on our earth when a being could have followed with his own eyes the gradual development of reptiles out of proto-amniotes, had he been able to be there at the time as an observer, endowed with a sufficiently long span of life.

---

* When Paulsen (on page 15 of the book mentioned above) says, "Different natural endowments and different conditions of life demand both a different bodily and also a different spiritual-moral diet," he is very close to the correct view, but yet he misses the decisive point. In so far as I am an individual, I need no diet. Dietetic means the art of bringing a particular specimen into harmony with its generic laws. But as an individual I am not a specimen of a general type.

166

Similarly, evolutionists ought to picture to themselves that a being could have watched the development of the solar system out of the Kant-Laplace primordial nebula, had he been able to remain in a suitable spot out in the cosmic world ether during that infinitely long time. That with such mental pictures, the nature of both the proto-amniotes and the Kant-Laplace cosmic nebula would have to be thought of *differently* from the way the materialist thinkers do, is here irrelevant. But no evolutionist should ever dream of maintaining that he could get the concept of the reptile, with all its characteristics, out of his concept of the proto-amniotic animal, if he had never seen a reptile. Just as little would it be possible to derive the solar system from the concept of the Kant-Laplace nebula, if this concept of a primordial nebula is thought of as being directly determined only by the percept of the primordial nebula. In other words, if the evolutionist is to think consistently, he is bound to maintain that later phases of evolution do actually result from earlier ones, and that once we have been given the concept of the imperfect *and* that of the perfect, we can see the connection; but on no account should he agree that the concept attained from the earlier is, in itself, sufficient for evolving the later out of it. From this it follows for ethics that, though we can certainly see the connection between later moral concepts and earlier, we cannot get even a single new moral idea out of the earlier ones. As a moral being, the individual produces his own content. For the student of ethics, the content thus produced is just as much a given thing as reptiles are a given thing for the scientist. Reptiles have developed out of proto-amniotes, but the scientist cannot get the concept of reptiles out of the concept of the proto-amniotes. Later moral ideas evolve out of earlier, but the student of ethics cannot get the moral concepts of a later civilization out of those of an earlier one. The confusion arises because, as scientists, we start with the facts before us, and then get to know them, whereas in moral action we ourselves first create the facts which we then get to know. In the process of evolution of the moral world order we accomplish something that, at a lower level, is accomplished by nature: we alter something perceptible. The ethical standard thus cannot start, like a law of nature, by being *known*, but only by being created. Only when it is there, can it become an object of knowledge.

But can we not then make the old a measure for the new? Is not every man compelled to measure the products of his moral imagination by the standard of traditional moral doctrines? For something that should reveal itself as morally productive, this would be just as absurd as to want to measure a new form in nature by an old one and say that, because reptiles do not conform to the proto-amniotes, they are an unjustifiable (pathological) form.

Ethical individualism, then, is not in opposition to a rightly understood theory of evolution, but follows directly from it. Haeckel's genealogical tree, from protozoa up to man as an organic being, ought to be capable of being continued without an interruption of natural law and without a break in the uniformity of evolution, up to the individual as a being that is moral in a definite sense. But on no account could the *nature* of a descendant species be deduced from the *nature* of an ancestral one. However true it is that the moral ideas of the individual have perceptibly developed out of those of his ancestors, it is equally true that the individual is morally barren unless he has moral ideas of his own.

The same ethical individualism that I have developed on the basis of views already given could also be derived from the theory of evolution. The final conviction would be the same; only the path by which it was reached would be different.

The appearance of completely new moral ideas through moral imagination is, for the theory of evolution, no more miraculous than the development of a new animal species out of an old one; only, as a monistic view of the world, this theory must reject, in morality as in science, every transcendental (metaphysical) influence, every influence that is merely inferred and cannot be experienced ideally. In doing so, the theory follows the same principle that guides it when it seeks the causes of new organic forms without invoking the interference of an extra-mundane Being who produces every new species, in accordance with a new creative thought, by supernatural influence. Just as monism has no use for supernatural creative thoughts in explaining living organisms, so it is equally impossible for it to derive the moral world order from causes which do not lie within the experienceable world. It cannot admit that the moral nature of will is completely accounted for by being traced back to a continuous supernatural influence upon moral life (divine government of the world from the outside), or to an act of revelation at a particular moment in history (giving of the ten commandments), or to God's appearance on the earth (as Christ). What happens to man, and in man, through all this, becomes a moral element only when, in human experience, it becomes an individual's own. For monism, moral processes are products of the world like everything else that exists, and their causes must be sought in the world, that is, in man, since man is the bearer of morality.

Ethical individualism, then, is the crowning feature of the edifice that Darwin and Haeckel have striven to build for natural science. It is spiritualized theory of evolution carried over into moral life.

Anyone who, in a narrow-minded way, restricts the concept of the *natural* from the outset to an arbitrarily limited sphere may easily conclude that there is no room in it for free individual action. The consistent evolutionist cannot fall a prey to such narrow-mindedness. He cannot let the natural course of evolution terminate with the ape, and allow man to have a "supernatural" origin; in his very search for the natural progenitors of man, he is bound to seek spirit in nature; again, he cannot stop short at the organic functions of man, and take only these as natural, but must go on to regard the free moral life as the spiritual continuation of organic life.

If he is to keep to his fundamental principles, the evolutionist can state only that the present form of moral action evolves from other forms of activity in the world; the characterizing of an action, that is, whether it is a *free* one, he must leave to the *immediate observation* of the action. In fact, he maintains only that men have developed out of ancestors that were not yet human. What men are actually like must be determined by observation of men themselves. The results of this observation cannot contradict the properly understood history of evolution. Only the assertion that the results are such as to exclude a natural ordering of the world would contradict recent trends in the natural sciences.*

Ethical individualism has nothing to fear from a natural science that understands itself: for observation shows that the perfect form of human action has *freedom* as its charac-

---

* That we speak of thoughts (ethical ideas) as objects of observation is fully justified. For, although during the activity of thinking the products of thinking do not appear at the same time in the field of observation, they can nevertheless become objects of observation afterwards. And it is in this way that we have arrived at our characterization of action.

teristic quality. This freedom must be allowed to the human will, in so far as the will realizes purely ideal intuitions. For these intuitions are not the results of a necessity acting upon them from without, but are due only to themselves. If a man finds that an action is the *image* of such an ideal intuition, then he feels it to be *free*. In this characteristic of an action lies its freedom.

What are we to say, from this standpoint, about the distinction mentioned earlier (page 8) between the two propositions, "To be free means to be able to *do* as one wills" and, "To be at liberty to desire or not to desire is the real proposition involved in the dogma of freewill"? Hamerling bases his view of free will precisely on this distinction, by declaring the first statement to be correct but the second to be an absurd tautology. He says, "I can *do* as I will. But to say I can want as I will is an empty tautology." Whether I am able to do, that is, to translate into reality, what I will, that is, what I have set before myself as my idea of action, depends on external circumstances and on my technical skill (see page 164). To be free means to be able of one's own accord to determine by moral imagination those mental pictures (motives) which underlie the action. Freedom is impossible if anything other then myself (mechanical process or merely inferred extra-mundane God) determines my moral ideas. In other words, I am free only when *I myself* produce these mental pictures, not when I am merely *able* to carry out the motives which another being has implanted in me. A free being is one who can *want* what he himself considers right. Whoever does anything other than what he wants must be impelled to it by motives which do not lie within him. Such a man is unfree in his action. To be at liberty to want what one considers right or what one considers wrong, would therefore mean to be at liberty to be free or unfree. This is, of course, just as absurd as to see freedom in the ability to do what one is compelled to will. But this last is just what Hamerling maintains when he says, "It is perfectly true that the will is always determined by motives, but it is absurd to say that on this account it is unfree; for a greater freedom can neither be desired nor conceived than the freedom to realize oneself in proportion to one's own strength and determination." Indeed it can! It is certainly possible to desire a greater freedom, and this for the first time the true one: namely, to decide for oneself the motives for one's will.

Under certain conditions a man may be induced to abandon the execution of his will. To allow others to prescribe to him what he *ought* to do—in other words, to want what another, and not he himself, considers right—to this a man will submit only to the extent that he does not feel *free*.

External powers may prevent me from doing as I will. Then they simply condemn me to do nothing or to be unfree. Not until they would enslave my spirit, drive my motives out of my head, and put their own motives in the place of mine, do they really aim at making me unfree. For this reason the Church sets itself not only against the mere *doing*, but especially against the *impure thoughts*, that is, the motives of my action. The Church makes me unfree if, for her, all those motives she has not herself enunciated seem impure. A Church or other community produces unfreedom when its priests or teachers make themselves into keepers of consciences, that is, when the faithful are *obliged* to go to them (to the confessional) for the motives of their actions.

Author's addition, 1918

In these chapters on the human will I have shown what man can experience in his actions so that, through this experience, he comes to be aware: My will is free. It is particularly significant that the right to call an act of will free arises from the experience that an ideal intuition comes to realization in the act of will. This experience *can* only be the result of an observation, and *is* so, in the sense that we observe our will on a path of development towards the goal where it becomes possible for an act of will to be sustained by purely ideal intuition. This goal can be reached, because in ideal intuition nothing else is at work but its own self-sustaining essence. When such an intuition is present in human consciousness, then it has not been developed out of the processes of the organism, but rather the organic activity has withdrawn to make room for the ideal activity (see page 121ff.). When I observe an act of will that is an image of an intuition, then from this act of will too all organically necessary activity has withdrawn. The act of will is free. This freedom of the will cannot be observed by anyone who is unable to see how the free act of will consists in the fact that, *firstly*, through the intuitive element, the activity that is necessary for the human organism is checked and repressed, and *then* replaced by the spiritual activity of the idea-filled will. Only those who cannot make *this* observation of the twofold nature of a free act of will, believe that *every* act of will is unfree. Those who can make this observation win through to the recognition that man is unfree in so far as he cannot complete the process of suppressing the organic activity; but that this unfreedom tends towards freedom, and that this freedom is by no means an abstract ideal but is a directive force inherent in human nature. Man is free to the extent that he is able to realize in his acts of will the same mood of soul that lives in him when he becomes aware of the forming of purely ideal (spiritual) intuitions.

CHAPTER THIRTEEN

The Value of Life
(Optimism and Pessimism)

A COUNTERPART to the question concerning the purpose of life, or the ordering of its destiny (see pages 156 ff.), is the question concerning its value. We meet here with two mutually opposed views, and between them all conceivable attempts at compromise. One view says that this world is the best that could conceivably exist, and that to live and to act in it is a blessing of untold value. Everything that exists displays harmonious and purposeful co-operation and is worthy of admiration. Even what is apparently bad and evil may, from a higher point of view, be seen to be good, for it represents an agreeable contrast with the good; we are the more able to appreciate the good when it is clearly contrasted with evil. Moreover, evil is not genuinely real; what we feel as evil is only a lesser degree of good. Evil is the absence of good; it has no significance in itself.

The other view maintains that life is full of misery and want; everywhere pain outweighs pleasure, sorrow outweighs joy. Existence is a burden, and non-existence would in all circumstances be preferable to existence.

The chief representatives of the former view, optimism, are Shaftesbury and Leibnitz; those of the latter, pessimism, are Schopenhauer and Eduard von Hartmann.

Leibnitz believes the world is the best of all possible worlds. A better one is impossible. For God is good and wise. A good God *wants* to create the best possible world; a wise God *knows* which is the best possible—He is able to distinguish the best from all other possible worse ones. Only an evil or an unwise God would be able to create a world worse than the best possible.

Whoever starts from this point of view will find it easy to lay down the direction that human action must follow in order to make its contribution to the greatest good of the world. All that man need do is to find out the counsels of God and to behave in accordance with them. If he knows what God's intentions are concerning the world and mankind, he will be able to do what is right. And he will be happy in the feeling that he is adding his share to the other good in the world. From this optimistic standpoint, then, life is worth living. It must stimulate us to co-operative participation.

Schopenhauer pictures things quite differently. He thinks of the foundation of the world not as an all-wise and all-beneficent being, but as blind urge or will. Eternal striving, ceaseless craving for satisfaction which is ever beyond reach, this is the fundamental characteristic of all active will. For no sooner is one goal attained, than a fresh need springs up, and so on. Satisfaction, when it occurs, lasts only for an infinitesimal time. The entire remaining content of our life is unsatisfied craving, that is, dissatisfaction and suffering. If at last blind craving is dulled, then all content is gone from our lives; an infinite boredom pervades our existence. Hence the best we can do is to stifle all wishes and needs within us and exterminate the will. Schopenhauer's pessimism leads to complete inactivity; his moral aim is *universal idleness*.

By a very different argument von Hartmann attempts to establish pessimism and to make use of it for ethics. He attempts, in keeping with a favourite tendency of our times, to base his world view on *experience*. From the *observation* of life he hopes to discover whether pleasure or pain outweighs the other in the world. He parades whatever appears to men as blessing and fortune before the tribunal of reason, in order to show that all alleged satisfaction turns out on closer inspection to be *illusion.* It is illusion when we believe that in health, youth, freedom, sufficient income, love (sexual satisfaction), pity, friendship and family life, self-respect, honour, fame, power, religious edification, pursuit of science and of art, hope of a life hereafter, participation in the progress of civilization—that in all these we have sources of happiness and satisfaction. Soberly considered, every enjoyment brings much more evil and misery into the world than pleasure. *The disagreeableness of the hangover is always greater than the agreeableness of getting drunk.* Pain far outweighs pleasure in the world. No man, even though relatively the happiest, would, if asked, wish to live through this miserable life a second time. Now, since Hartmann does not deny the presence of an ideal factor (wisdom) in the world, but rather gives it equal standing with blind urge (will), he can credit his primal Being with the creation of the world only if he allows the pain in the world to serve a wise world-purpose. The pain of created beings is, however, nothing but God's pain itself, for the life of the world as a whole is identical with the life of God. An all-wise Being can, however, see his goal only in release from suffering, and, since all existence is suffering, in release from existence. To transform existence into the far better state of non-existence is the purpose of all creation. The course of the world is a continuous battle against God's pain, which ends at last with the annihilation of all existence. The moral life of men, therefore, will consist in taking part in the annihilation of existence. God has created the world so that through it He may free Himself from His infinite pain. The world is "to be regarded, more or less, as an itching eruption upon the Absolute," by means of which the unconscious healing power of the

Absolute rids itself of an inward disease, "or even as a painful poultice which the All-One applies to himself in order first to divert the inner pain outwards, and then to get rid of it altogether." Human beings are integral parts of the world. In them God suffers. He has created them in order to disperse His infinite pain. The pain which each one of us suffers is but a drop in the infinite ocean of God's pain.*

Man has to permeate his whole being with the recognition that the pursuit of individual satisfaction (egoism) is a folly, and that he ought to be guided solely by the task of dedicating himself to the redemption of God by unselfish devotion to the progress of the world. Thus, in contrast to Schopenhauer's, von Hartmann's pessimism leads us to activity devoted to a sublime task.

But is it really based on experience?

To strive for satisfaction means that our activity reaches out beyond the actual content of our lives. A creature is hungry, that is, it strives for repletion, when its organic functions, if they are to continue, demand the supply of fresh means of life in the form of nourishment. The striving for honour means that a man only regards what he personally does or leaves undone as valuable when his activity is approved by others. The striving for knowledge arises when a man finds that something is missing from the world that he sees, hears, and so on, as long as he has not understood it. The fulfilment of the striving creates pleasure in the striving individual, failure creates pain. It is important here to observe that pleasure and pain are dependent only upon the fulfilment or non-fulfilment of my striving. The striving itself can by no means be counted as pain. Hence, if it happens that in the very moment in which a striving is fulfilled a new

* Hartmann, *Phaenomenologie des sittlichen Bewusstseins*, pp. 866 ff.

striving at once arises, this is no ground for saying that, because in every case enjoyment gives rise to a desire for its repetition or for a fresh pleasure, my pleasure has given birth to pain. I can speak of pain only when desire runs up against the impossibility of fulfilment. Even when an enjoyment that I have had creates in me the desire for the experience of greater or more refined pleasure, I cannot speak of this desire as a pain created by the previous pleasure until the means of experiencing the greater or more refined pleasure fail me. Only when pain appears as a natural consequence of pleasure, as for instance when a woman's sexual pleasure is followed by the suffering of childbirth and the cares of a family, can I find in the enjoyment the originator of the pain. If striving by itself called forth pain, then each reduction of striving would have to be accompanied by pleasure. But the opposite is the case. To have no striving in one's life creates boredom, and this is connected with displeasure. Now, since it may be a long time before striving meets with fulfilment, and since, in the interval, it is content with the hope of fulfilment, we must acknowledge that the pain has nothing whatever to do with the striving as such, but depends solely on the non-fulfilment of the striving. Schopenhauer, then, is in any case wrong to take desiring or striving (will) as being in itself the source of pain.

In fact, just the opposite is correct. Striving (desiring) in itself gives pleasure. Who does not know the enjoyment given by the hope of a remote but intensely desired goal? This joy is the companion of all labour that gives us its fruits only in the future. It is a pleasure quite independent of the attainment of the goal. For when the goal has been reached, the pleasure of fulfilment is added as something new to the pleasure of striving. If anyone were to argue that the pain caused by an unsatisfied aim is increased by the pain of disappointed hope, and that thus, in the end, the pain of non-fulfilment will eventually outweigh the possible pleasure of fulfilment, we shall have to reply that the reverse may be the case, and that the recollection of past enjoyment at a time of unfulfilled desire will just as often mitigate the pain of non-fulfilment. Whoever exclaims in the face of shattered hopes, "I have done my part," is a proof of this assertion. The blissful feeling of having tried one's best is overlooked by those who say of every unsatisfied desire that not only is the joy of fulfilment absent but the enjoyment of the desiring itself has been destroyed.

The fulfilment of a desire brings pleasure and its non-fulfilment brings pain. But from this we must not conclude that pleasure is the satisfaction of a desire, and pain its non-satisfaction. Both pleasure and pain can be experienced without being the consequence of desire. Illness is pain not preceded by desire. If anyone were to maintain that illness is unsatisfied desire for health, he would be making the mistake of regarding the unconscious wish not to fall ill, which we all take for granted, as a positive desire. When someone receives a legacy from a rich relative of whose existence he had not the faintest idea, this fills him with pleasure without any preceding desire.

Hence, if we set out to enquire whether the balance is on the side of pleasure or of pain, we must take into account the pleasure of desiring, the pleasure at the fulfilment of a desire, and the pleasure which comes to us without any striving. On the other side of the account we shall have to enter the displeasure of boredom, the pain of unfulfilled striving, and lastly the pain which comes to us without any desiring on our part. Under this last heading we shall have to put also the displeasure caused by work, not chosen by ourselves, that has been forced upon us.

This leads to the question: What is the right method for striking the *balance* between these *credit* and *debit* columns? Eduard von Hartmann believes that it is reason that holds the scales. It is true that he says, "Pain and pleasure *exist* only in so far as they are actually *felt*."* It follows that there can be no yardstick for pleasure other than the subjective one of feeling. I must *feel* whether the sum of my disagreeable feelings together with my agreeable feelings leaves me with a balance of pleasure or of pain. But for all that, von Hartmann maintains that, "though the value of the life of every person can be set down only according to his own subjective measure, yet it by no means follows that every person is able to arrive at the *correct* algebraic sum from all the collected emotions in his life—or, in other words, that *his total estimate* of his own life, with regard to his subjective experiences, would be correct." With this, the *rational estimation* of feeling is once more made the evaluator.†

Anyone who follows fairly closely the line of thought of such thinkers as Eduard von Hartmann may believe it necessary, in order to arrive at a correct valuation of life, to clear out of the way those factors which falsify our *judgment* about the balance of pleasure and pain. He can try to do this in two ways. *Firstly*, by showing that our desire (instinct, will) interferes with our sober estimation of feeling values in a disturbing way. Whereas, for instance, we ought to say to ourselves that sexual enjoyment is a source of evil, we are misled by the fact that the sexual instinct is very strong in

* *Philosophie des Unbewussten*, 7th edition, Vol. II, p. 290.
† Those who want to settle *by calculation* whether the sum total of pleasure or that of pain is the bigger, ignore that they are subjecting to calculation something which is nowhere experienced. Feeling does not calculate, and what matters for the real valuing of life is what we really experience, not what results from an imaginary calculation.

us into conjuring up the prospect of a pleasure which just is not there in that degree at all. We want to enjoy ourselves; hence we do not admit to ourselves that we suffer under the enjoyment. *Secondly*, he can do it by subjecting feelings to a critical examination and attempting to prove that the objects to which our feelings attach themselves are revealed as illusions by the light of reason, and that *they are destroyed from the moment that our ever growing intelligence sees through the illusions.*

He can think of the matter in the following way. If an ambitious man wants to determine clearly whether, up to the moment of his enquiry, there has been a surplus of pleasure or of pain in his life, then he has to free himself from two sources of error that may affect his judgment. Being ambitious, this fundamental feature of his character will make him see the joys due to the recognition of his achievements through a magnifying glass, and the humiliations due to his rebuffs through a diminishing glass. At the time when he suffered the rebuffs he felt the humiliations just because he was ambitious; in recollection they appear to him in a milder light, whereas the joys of recognition to which he is so susceptible leave a far deeper impression. Now, for an ambitious man it is an undeniable blessing that it should be so. The deception diminishes his pain in the moment of self-analysis. None the less, his judgment is wrong. The sufferings over which a veil is now drawn were actually experienced by him in all their intensity, and hence he enters them at a wrong valuation in his life's account book. In order to arrive at a correct estimate, an ambitious man would have to lay aside his ambition for the time of his enquiry. He would have to review his past life without any distorting glasses before his mind's eye. Otherwise he would resemble a merchant who, in making up his books, enters among the items on the credit side his own zeal in business.

But the holder of this view can go even further. He can say: The ambitious man will even make clear to himself that the recognition he pursues is a worthless thing. Either by himself, or through the influence of others, he will come to see that for an intelligent man recognition by others counts for very little, seeing that "in all such matters, other than those that are questions of sheer existence or that are already finally settled by science," one can be quite sure "that the majority is wrong and the minority right. . . . Whoever makes ambition the lode-star of his life puts his life's happiness at the mercy of such a judgment."* If the ambitious man admits all this to himself, then he must regard as illusion what his ambition had pictured as reality, and thus also the feelings attached to these illusions of his ambition. On this basis it could then be said that such feelings of pleasure as are produced by illusion must also be struck out of the balance sheet of life's values; what then remains represents the sum total of life's pleasures stripped of all illusion, and this is so small compared with the sum total of pain that life is no joy and non-existence preferable to existence.

But while it is immediately evident that the deception produced by the instinct of ambition leads to a false result when striking the balance of pleasure, we must none the less challenge what has been said about the recognition of the illusory character of the objects of pleasure. The elimination from the credit side of life of all pleasurable feelings which accompany actual or supposed illusions would positively falsify the balance of pleasure and pain. For an ambitious man has genuinely enjoyed the acclamations of the multitude, irrespective of whether subsequently he himself, or some other person, recognizes that this acclamation is an illusion.

* *Philosophie des Unbewussten*, Vol. II, p. 332.

The pleasant sensation he has had is not in the least diminished by this recognition. The elimination of all such "illusory" feelings from life's balance does not make our judgment about our feelings more correct, but rather obliterates from life feelings which were actually there.

And why should these feelings be eliminated? For whoever has them, they are certainly pleasure-giving; for whoever has conquered them, a purely mental but none the less significant pleasure arises through the experience of self-conquest (not through the vain emotion: What a noble fellow I am! but through the objective sources of pleasure which lie in the self-conquest). If we strike out feelings from the pleasure side of the balance on the ground that they are attached to objects which turn out to have been illusory, we make the value of life dependent not on the quantity but on the quality of pleasure, and this, in turn, on the value of the objects which cause the pleasure. But if I want to determine the value of life in the first place by the quantity of pleasure or pain which it brings, I may not presuppose something else which already determines the positive or negative value of the pleasure. If I say I want to compare the quantity of pleasure with the quantity of pain in order to see which is greater, I am bound to bring into my account all pleasures and pains in their actual intensities, whether they are based on illusions or not. Whoever ascribes a lesser value for life to a pleasure which is based on an illusion than to one which can justify itself before the tribunal of reason, makes the value of life dependent on factors other than pleasure.

Whoever puts down pleasure as less valuable when it is attached to a worthless object, resembles a merchant who enters the considerable profits of a toy factory in his account at a quarter of their actual amount on the ground that the factory produces nothing but playthings for children.

If the point is simply to weigh quantity of pleasure against quantity of pain, then the illusory character of the objects causing certain feelings of pleasure must be left right out of the question.

The method recommended by von Hartmann, that is, rational consideration of the quantities of pleasure and pain produced by life, has thus led us to the point where we know how we are to set out our accounts, what we are to put down on the one side of our book and what on the other. But how is the calculation now to be made? Is reason actually capable of striking the balance?

A merchant has made a mistake in his reckoning if his *calculated* profit does not agree with the demonstrable results or expectations of his business. Similarly, the philosopher will undoubtedly have made a mistake in his estimate if he cannot demonstrate in actual feeling the surplus of pleasure, or pain, that he has somehow extracted from his accounts.

For the present I shall not look into the calculations of those pessimists whose opinion of the world is measured by reason; but if one is to decide whether to carry on the business of life or not, one will first demand to be shown where the alleged surplus of pain is to be found.

Here we touch the point where reason is *not* in a position to determine by itself the surplus of pleasure or of pain, but where it must demonstrate this surplus as a percept in life. For man reaches reality not through concepts alone but through the interpenetration of concepts and percepts (and feelings are percepts) which thinking brings about (see page 67 ff.). A merchant, after all, will give up his business only when the losses calculated by his accountant are confirmed by the facts. If this does not happen, he gets his accountant to make the calculation over again. That is exactly what a man will do in the business of life. If a philosopher wants to prove to him that the pain is far greater than the pleasure, but he himself does not feel it to be so, then he will reply, "You have gone astray in your reckoning; think it all out again." But should there come a time in a business when the losses are really so great that the firm's credit no longer suffices to satisfy the creditors, then bankruptcy will result if the merchant fails to keep himself informed about the state of his affairs by careful accounting. Similarly, if the quantity of pain in a man's life became at any time so great that no hope of future pleasure (credit) could help him to get over the pain, then the bankruptcy of life's business would inevitably follow.

Now the number of those who kill themselves is relatively unimportant when compared with the multitude of those who live bravely on. Only very few men give up the business of life because of the pain involved. What follows from this? Either that it is untrue to say that the quantity of pain is greater than the quantity of pleasure, or that we do not at all make the continuation of life dependent on the quantity of pleasure or pain that is felt.

In a very curious way, Eduard von Hartmann's pessimism comes to the conclusion that life is valueless because it contains a surplus of pain and yet affirms the necessity of going on with it. This necessity lies in the fact that the world purpose mentioned above (page 177) can be achieved only by the ceaseless, devoted labour of human beings. But as long as men still pursue their egotistical cravings they are unfit for such selfless labour. Not until they have convinced themselves through experience and reason that the pleasures of life pursued by egoism cannot be attained, do they devote themselves to their proper tasks. In this way the pessimistic conviction is supposed to be the source of unselfishness. An education based on pessimism should exterminate egoism by making it see the hopelessness of its case.

According to this view, then, the striving for pleasure is inherent in human nature from the outset. Only when fulfilment is seen to be impossible does this striving retire in favour of higher tasks for mankind.

It cannot be said that egoism is overcome in the true sense of the word by an ethical world conception that expects a devotion to unselfish aims in life through the acceptance of pessimism. The moral ideals are said not to be strong enough to dominate the will until man has learnt that selfish striving after pleasure cannot lead to any satisfaction. Man, whose selfishness desires the grapes of pleasure, finds them sour because he cannot reach them, and so he turns his back on them and devotes himself to an unselfish way of life. Moral ideals, then, according to the opinion of pessimists, are not strong enough to overcome egoism; but they establish their dominion on the ground previously cleared for them by the recognition of the hopelessness of egoism.

If men by nature were to strive after pleasure but were unable to reach it, then annihilation of existence, and salvation through non-existence, would be the only rational goal. And if one holds the view that the real bearer of the pain of the world is God, then man's task would consist in bringing about the salvation of God. Through the suicide of the individual, the realization of this aim is not advanced, but hindered. Rationally, God can only have created men in order to bring about his salvation through their actions. Otherwise creation would be purposeless. And it is extra-human purposes that such a world conception has in mind. Each one of us has to perform his own particular task in the general work of salvation. If he withdraws from the task by suicide, then the work which was intended for him must be done by another. Somebody else must bear the torment of existence in his stead. And since within every being it is God who actually bears all pain, the suicide does not in the least diminish the quantity of God's pain, but rather imposes upon God the additional difficulty of providing a substitute.

All this presupposes that pleasure is the yardstick for the value of life. Now life manifests itself through a number of instinctive desires (needs). If the value of life depended on its producing more pleasure than pain, an instinct which brought to its owner a balance of pain would have to be called valueless. Let us, therefore, examine instinct and pleasure to see whether the former can be measured by the latter. In order not to arouse the suspicion that we consider life to begin only at the level of "aristocracy of the intellect", we shall begin with the "purely animal" need, hunger.

Hunger arises when our organs are unable to continue their proper function without a fresh supply of food. What a hungry man wants first of all is to satisfy his hunger. As soon as the supply of nourishment has reached the point where hunger ceases, everything that the instinct for food craves has been attained. The enjoyment that comes with being satisfied consists primarily in putting an end to the pain caused by hunger. But to the mere instinct for food a further need is added. For man does not merely desire to repair the disturbance in the functioning of his organs by the consumption of food, or to overcome the pain of hunger; he seeks to effect this to the accompaniment of pleasurable sensations of taste. If he feels hungry and is within half an hour of an appetizing meal, he may even refuse inferior food, which could satisfy him sooner, so as not to spoil his appetite for the better fare to come. He needs hunger in order to get the full enjoyment from his meal. Thus for him hunger becomes at the same time a cause of pleasure. Now if all the existing hunger in the world could be satisfied, we should then have the total quantity of enjoyment attributable to the presence of the need for nourishment. To this would still have to be added the special pleasure which the gourmet achieves by cultivating his palate beyond the common measure.

This quantity of pleasure would reach the highest conceivable value if no need aiming at the kind of enjoyment under consideration remained unsatified, and if with the enjoyment we had not to accept a certain amount of pain into the bargain.

Modern science holds the view that nature produces more life than it can sustain, that is to say, more hunger than it is able to satisfy. The surplus of life thus produced must perish in pain in the struggle for existence. Admittedly the needs of life at every moment in the course of the world are greater than the available means of satisfaction, and that the enjoyment of life is affected as a result. Such enjoyment as actually does occur, however, is not in the least reduced. Wherever a desire is satisfied, the corresponding quantity of pleasure exists, even though in the desiring creature itself or in its fellows there are plenty of unsatisfied instincts. What is, however, diminished by all this is the *value* of the enjoyment of life. If only a part of the needs of a living creature finds satisfaction, it experiences a corresponding degree of enjoyment. This pleasure has a lower value, the smaller it is in proportion to the total demands of life in the field of the desires in question. One can represent this value by a fraction, of which the numerator is the pleasure actually experienced while the denominator is the sum total of needs. This fraction has the value 1 when the numerator and the denominator are equal, that is, when all needs are fully satisfied. The fraction becomes greater than 1 when a creature experiences more pleasure than its desires demand; and it becomes smaller than 1 when the quantity of pleasure falls short of the sum total of desires. But the fraction can never become *zero* as long as the numerator has any value at all, however small. If a man were to make up a final account before his death, and were to think of the quantity of enjoyment connected with a particular instinct (for example, hunger) as being distributed over the whole of his life together with all the demands made by this instinct, then the pleasure experienced might perhaps have a very small value, but it could never become valueless. If the quantity of pleasure remains constant, then, with an increase in the needs of the creature, the value of the pleasure diminishes. The same is true for the sum of life in nature. The greater the number of creatures in proportion to those which are able to satisfy their instincts fully, the smaller is the average value of pleasure in life. The cheques on life's pleasure which are drawn in our favour in the form of our instincts, become less valuable if we cannot expect to cash them for the full amount. If I get enough to eat for three days and as a result must then go hungry for another three days, the actual pleasure on the three days of eating is not thereby diminished. But I have now to think of it as distributed over six days, and thus its *value* for my food-instinct is reduced by half. In just the same way the magnitude of pleasure is related to the *degree* of my need. If I am hungry enough for two pieces of bread and can only get one, the pleasure I derive from it had only half the value it would have had if the eating of it has satisfied my hunger. This is the way that the *value* of a pleasure is determined in life. It is measured by the needs of life. Our desires are the yardstick; pleasure is the thing that is measured. The enjoyment of satisfying hunger has a value only because hunger exists; and it has a value of a definite magnitude through the proportion it bears to the magnitude of the existing hunger. Unfulfilled demands of our life throw their shadow even upon satisfied desires, and thus detract from the *value* of pleasurable hours. But we can also speak of the *present value* of a feeling of pleasure. This value is the lower, the smaller the pleasure is in proportion to the duration and intensity of our desire.

A quantity of pleasure has its full value for us when in duration and degree it exactly coincides with our desire. A quantity of pleasure which is smaller than our desire diminishes the value of the pleasure; a quantity which is greater produces a surplus which has not been demanded and which is felt as pleasure only so long as, whilst enjoying the pleasure, we can increase the intensity of our desire. If the increase in our desire is unable to keep pace with the increase in pleasure, then pleasure turns into displeasure. The thing that would otherwise satisfy us now assails us without our wanting it and makes us suffer. This proves that pleasure has value for us only to the extent that we can measure it against our desires. An excess of pleasurable feeling turns into pain. This may be observed especially in people whose desire for a particular kind of pleasure is very small. In people whose instinct for food is stunted, eating readily becomes nauseating. This again shows that desire is the standard by which we measure the value of pleasure.

Now the pessimist might say that an unsatisfied instinct for food brings into the world not only displeasure at the lost enjoyment, but also positive pain, misery and want. He can base this statement upon the untold misery of starving people and upon the vast amount of suffering which arises indirectly for such people from their lack of food. And if he wants to extend his assertion to nature outside man as well, he can point to the suffering of animals that die of starvation at certain times of the year. The pessimist maintains that these evils far outweigh the amount of pleasure that the instinct for food brings into the world.

There is indeed no doubt that one can compare *pleasure* and *pain* and can estimate the surplus of one or the other much as we do in the case of *profit* and *loss*. But if the pessimist believes that because there is a surplus of pain he can conclude that life is valueless, he falls into the error of making a calculation that in real life is never made.

Our desire, in any given case, is directed to a particular object. As we have seen, the value of the pleasure of satisfaction will be the greater, the greater is the amount of pleasure in relation to the intensity of our desire.* On this intensity of desire also will depend how much pain we are willing to bear as part of the price of achieving the pleasure. We compare the quantity of pain not with the quantity of pleasure but with the intensity of our desire. If someone takes great delight in eating, he will, by reason of his enjoyment in better times, find it easier to bear a period of hunger than will someone for whom eating is no pleasure. A woman who wants to have a child compares the pleasure that would come from possessing it not with the amount of pain due to pregnancy, childbirth, nursing and so on, but with her desire to possess the child.

We never aim at a certain quantity of pleasure in the abstract, but at concrete satisfaction in a perfectly definite way. If we are aiming at a pleasure which must be satisfied by a particular object or a particular sensation, we shall not be satisfied with some other object or some other sensation that gives us an equal amount of pleasure. If we are aiming at satisfying our hunger, we cannot replace the pleasure this

* We disregard here the case where excessive increase of pleasure turns pleasure into pain.

would give us by a pleasure equally great, but produced by going for a walk. Only if our desire were, quite generally, for a certain fixed quantity of pleasure as such, would it disappear as soon as the price of achieving it were seen to be a still greater quantity of pain. But since satisfaction of a particular kind is being aimed at, fulfilment brings the pleasure even when, along with it, a still greater pain has to be taken into the bargain. But because the instincts of living creatures move in definite directions and go after concrete goals, the quantity of pain endured on the way to the goal cannot be set down as an equivalent factor in our calculations. Provided the desire is sufficiently intense to be present in some degree after having overcome the pain—however great that pain in itself may be—then the pleasure of satisfaction can still be tasted to the full. The desire, therefore, does not compare the pain directly to the pleasure achieved, but compares it indirectly by relating its own intensity to that of the pain. The question is not whether the pleasure to be gained is greater than the pain, but whether the desire for the goal is greater than the hindering effect of the pain involved. If the hindrance is greater than the desire, then the desire gives way to the inevitable, weakens and strives no further. Since our demand is for satisfaction in a particular way, the pleasure connected with it acquires a significance such that, once we have achieved satisfaction, we need take the quantity of pain into account only to the extent that it has reduced the intensity of our desire. If I am a passionate admirer of beautiful views, I never calculate the amount of pleasure which the view from the mountain top gives me as compared directly with the pain of the toilsome ascent and descent; but I reflect whether, after having overcome all difficulties, my desire for the view will still be sufficiently intense. Only indirectly, through the intensity of the desire, can pleasure and pain together lead to a result. Therefore the question is not at all whether there is a surplus of pleasure or of pain, but whether the will for pleasure is strong enough to overcome the pain.

A proof for the correctness of this statement is the fact that we put a higher value on pleasure when it has to be purchased at the price of great pain than when it falls into our lap like a gift from heaven. When suffering and misery have toned down our desire and yet after all our goal is reached, then the pleasure, *in proportion* to the amount of desire still left, is *all the greater*. Now, as I have shown (page 189), this proportion represents the *value* of the pleasure. A further proof is given through the fact that living creatures (including man) give expression to their instincts as long as they are able to bear the pain and misery involved. The struggle for existence is but a consequence of this fact. All existing life strives to express itself, and only that part of it whose desires are smothered by the over-whelming weight of difficulties abandons the struggle. Every living creature seeks food until lack of food destroys its life. Man, too, does not turn his hand against himself until he believes, rightly or wrongly, that those aims in life that are worth his striving are beyond his reach. So long as he still believes in the possibility of reaching what, in his view, is worth striving for, he will battle against all misery and pain. Philosophy would first have to convince him that an act of will makes sense only when the pleasure is greater than the pain; for by nature he will strive for the objects of his desire if he can bear the necessary pain, however great it may be. But such a philosophy would be mistaken because it would make the human will dependent on a circumstance (the surplus of pleasure over pain) which is originally foreign to man. The original measure of his will is desire, and desire asserts itself as long as it can. When it is a question of pleasure and pain in the satisfaction of a desire, the calculation that is made, not in philosophical theory, but in *life*, can be compared with the following. If in buying a certain quantity of apples I am obliged to take twice as many rotten ones as sound ones—because the seller wants to clear his stock—I shall not hesitate for one moment to accept the bad apples as well, if the smaller quantity of good ones are worth so much to me that in addition to their purchase price I am also prepared to bear the expense of disposing of the bad ones. This example illustrates the relation between the quantities of pleasure and pain resulting from an instinct. I determine the value of the good apples not by subtracting the total number of the good ones from that of the bad ones but by assessing whether the good ones still have value for me in spite of the presence of the bad ones.

Just as I leave the bad apples out of account in the enjoyment of the good ones, so I give myself up to the satisfaction of a desire after having shaken off the unavoidable pain.

Even if pessimism were right in its assertion that there is more pain then pleasure in the world, this would have no influence on the will, since living creatures would still strive after the pleasure that remains. The empirical proof that pain outweighs joy (if such proof could be given) would certainly be effective for showing up the futility of the school of philosophy that sees the value of life in a surplus of pleasure (eudæmonism) but not for showing that the will, as such, is irrational; for the will is not set upon a surplus of pleasure, but upon the amount of pleasure that remains after getting over the pain. This still appears as a goal worth striving for.

Some have tried to refute pessimism by stating that it is impossible to calculate the surplus of pleasure or of pain in the world. That any calculation can be done at all depends on whether the things to be calculated can be compared in respect of their magnitudes. Every pain and every pleasure has a definite magnitude (intensity and duration). Further, we can compare pleasurable feelings of different kinds one with another, at least approximately, with regard to their magnitudes. We know whether we derive more entertainment from a good cigar or from a good joke. Therefore there can be no objection to comparing different sorts of pleasure and pain in respect of their magnitudes. And the investigator who sets himself the task of determining the surplus of pleasure or pain in the world starts from fully justified assumptions. One may declare the conclusions of pessimism to be false, but one cannot doubt that quantities of pleasure and pain can be scientifically estimated, and the balance of pleasure thereby determined. It is, however, quite wrong to claim that the result of this calculation has any consequences for the human will. The cases where we really make the value of our activity dependent on whether pleasure or pain shows a surplus are those where the objects towards which our activity is directed are all the same to us. If it is only a question whether, after the day's work, I am to amuse myself by a game or by light conversation, and if I am totally indifferent to what I do as long as it serves the purpose, then I simply ask myself: What gives me the greatest surplus of pleasure? And I shall most certainly abandon the activity if the scales incline towards the side of displeasure. If we are buying a toy for a child we consider, in selecting, what will give him the greatest happiness. In all other cases we do not base our decision exclusively on the balance of pleasure.

Therefore, if the pessimists believe that by showing pain to be present in greater quantity than pleasure they are preparing the ground for unselfish devotion to the work of civilization, they forget that the human will, by its very nature, does not allow itself to be influenced by this knowledge. Human striving is directed towards the measure of satisfaction that is possible after all difficulties are overcome. Hope of such satisfaction is the foundation of all human activity. The work of every individual and of the whole of civilization springs from this hope. Pessimistic ethics believes that it must present the pursuit of happiness as an impossibility for man in order that he may devote himself to his proper moral tasks. But these moral tasks are nothing but the concrete natural and spiritual instincts; and man strives to satisfy them in spite of the incidental pain. The pursuit of happiness which the pessimist would eradicate is therefore nowhere to be found. But the tasks which man has to fulfil, he does fulfil, because from the very nature of his being he *wants* to fulfil them, once he has properly recognized their nature. Pessimistic ethics declares that only when a man has given up the quest for pleasure can he devote himself to what he recognizes as his task in life. But no system of ethics can ever invent any life tasks other than the realization of the satisfactions that human desires demand and the fulfilment of man's moral ideals. No ethics can deprive man of the pleasure he experiences in the fulfilment of his desires. When the pessimist says, "Do not strive for pleasure, for you can never attain it; strive rather for what you recognize to be your task," we must reply, "But this is just what man does, and the notion that he strives merely for happiness is no more than the invention of an errant philosophy." He aims at the satisfaction of what he himself desires, and he has in view the concrete objects of his striving, not "happiness" in the abstract; and fulfilment is for him a pleasure. When pessimistic ethics demands, "Strive not for pleasure, but for the attainment of what you see as your life's task," it hits on the very thing that man, in his own being, *wants*. Man does not need to be turned inside out by philosophy, he does not need to discard his human nature, before he can be moral. Morality lies in striving for a goal that one recognizes as justified; it is human nature to pursue it as long as the pain incurred does not inhibit the desire for it altogether. This is the essence of all genuine will. Ethical behaviour is not based upon the eradication of all striving for pleasure to the end that bloodless abstract ideas may establish their dominion unopposed by any strong yearnings for the enjoyment of life, but rather upon a *strong will* sustained by ideal intuitions, a will that reaches its goal even though the path be thorny.

Moral ideals spring from the moral imagination of man. Their realization depends on his desire for them being intense enough to overcome pain and misery. They are *his* intuitions, the driving forces which his spirit harnesses; he *wants* them, because their realization is his highest pleasure. He needs no ethics to forbid him to strive for pleasure and then to tell him what he *shall* strive for. He will strive for moral ideals if his moral imagination is sufficiently active to provide him with intuitions that give his will the strength to make its way against all the obstacles inherent in his constitution, including the pain that is necessarily involved.

If a man strives for sublimely great ideals, it is because they are the content of his own being, and their realization will bring him a joy compared to which the pleasure that a limited outlook gets from the gratification of commonplace desires is a mere triviality. Idealists *revel*, spiritually, in the translation of their ideals into reality.

Anyone who would eradicate the pleasure brought by the fulfilment of human desires will first have to make man a slave who acts not because he wants to but only because he must. For the achievement of what one wanted to do gives pleasure. What we call *good* is not what a man *must* do but what he will *want* to do if he develops the true nature of man to the full. Anyone who does not acknowledge this must first drive out of man all that man himself wants to do, and then, *from outside*, prescribe the content he is to give to his will.

Man values the fulfilment of a desire because the desire springs from his own being. What is achieved has its value because it has been wanted. If we deny any value to what man himself wants, then aims that do have value will have to be found in something that man does not want.

An ethics built on pessimism arises from the disregard of moral imagination. Only if one considers that the individual human spirit is itself incapable of giving content to its striving can one expect the craving for pleasure to account fully for all acts of will. A man without imagination creates no moral ideas. They must be given to him. Physical nature sees to it that he strives to satisfy his lower desires. But the development of the *whole* man also includes those desires that originate in the spirit. Only if one believes that man has no such spiritual desires can one declare that he must receive them from without. Then one would also be entitled to say that it is man's duty to do what he does not want. Every ethical system that demands of man that he should suppress his own will in order to fulfil tasks that he does not want, reckons not with the *whole* man but with one in which the faculty of spiritual desire is lacking. For a man who is harmoniously developed, the so-called ideals of virtue lie, not *without*, but *within* the sphere of his own being. Moral action consists not in the eradication of a one-sided personal will but in the *full* development of human nature. Those who hold that moral ideals are attainable only if man destroys his own personal will, are not aware that these ideals are wanted by man just as he wants the satisfaction of the so-called animal instincts.

It cannot be denied that the views here outlined may easily be misunderstood. Immature people without moral imagination like to look upon the instincts of their half-developed natures as the fullest expression of the human race, and reject all moral ideas which they have not themselves produced, in order that they may "live themselves out" undisturbed. But it goes without saying that what is right for a fully developed human being does not hold good for half-developed human natures. Anyone who still needs to be educated to the point where his moral nature breaks through the husk of his lower passions, will not have the same things expected of him as of a mature person. However, it was not my intention to show what needs to be impressed upon an undeveloped person, but what lies within the essential nature of a mature human being. My intention was to demonstrate the possibility of freedom, and freedom is manifested not in actions performed under constraint of sense or soul but in actions sustained by spiritual intuitions.

The mature man gives himself his own value. He does not aim at pleasure, which comes to him as a gift of grace on the part of Nature or of the Creator; nor does he fulfil an abstract duty which he recognizes as such after he has renounced the striving for pleasure. He acts as he wants to act, that is, in accordance with the standard of his ethical intuitions; and he finds in the achievement of what he wants the true enjoyment of life. He determines the value of life by measuring achievements against aims. An ethics which replaces "would" with mere "should", inclination with mere duty, will consequently determine the value of man by measuring his fulfilment of duty against the demands that it makes. It measures man with a yardstick external to his own being.

The view which I have here developed refers man back to himself. It recognizes as the true value of life only what each individual regards as such, according to the standard of his own will. It no more acknowledges a value of life that is not recognized by the individual than it does a purpose of life that has not originated in him. It sees in the individual who knows himself through and through, his own master and his own assessor.

Author's addition, 1918

The argument of this chapter will be misunderstood if one is caught by the apparent objection that the will, as such, is the irrational factor in man and that once this irrationality is made clear to him he will see that the goal of his ethical striving must lie in ultimate emancipation from the will. An apparent objection of exactly this kind was brought against me from a reputable quarter in that I was told that it is the business of the philosopher to make good just what lack of thought leads animals and most men to neglect, namely, to strike a proper balance of life's account. But this objection just misses the main point. If freedom is to be realized, the will in human nature must be sustained by intuitive thinking; at the same time, however, we find that an act of will may also be determined by factors other than intuition, though *only* in the free realization of intuitions issuing from man's essential nature do we find morality and its value. Ethical individualism is well able to present morality in its full dignity, for it sees true morality not in what brings about the agreement of an act of will with a standard of behaviour in an external way, but in what arises in man when he develops his moral will as an integral part of his whole being so that to do what is not moral appears to him as a stunting and crippling of his nature.

CHAPTER FOURTEEN

Individuality and Genus

THE view that man is destined to become a complete, self-contained, free individuality seems to be contested by the fact that he makes his appearance as a member of a naturally given totality (race, people, nation, family, male or female sex) and also works within a totality (state, church, and so on). He bears the general characteristics of the group to which he belongs, and he gives to his actions a content that is determined by the position he occupies among many others.

This being so, is individuality possible at all? Can we regard man as a totality in himself, seeing that he grows out of one totality and integrates himself into another?

Each member of a totality is determined, as regards its characteristics and functions, by the whole totality. A racial group is a totality and all the people belonging to it bear the characteristic features that are inherent in the nature of the group. How the single member is constituted, and how he will behave, are determined by the character of the racial group. Therefore the physiognomy and conduct of the individual have something generic about them. If we ask why some particular thing about a man is like this or like that, we are referred back from the individual to the genus. The genus explains why something in the individual appears in the form we observe.

Man, however, makes himself free from what is generic. For the generic features of the human race, when rightly understood, do not restrict man's freedom, and should not artificially be made to do so. A man develops qualities and activities of his own, and the basis for these we can seek only in the man himself. What is generic in him serves only as a medium in which to express his own individual being. He uses as a foundation the characteristics that nature has given him, and to these he gives a form appropriate to his own being. If we seek in the generic laws the reasons for an expression of this being, we seek in vain. We are concerned with something purely individual which can be explained only in terms of itself. If a man has achieved this emancipation from all that is generic, and we are nevertheless determined to explain everything about him in generic terms, then we have no sense for what is individual.

It is impossible to understand a human being completely if one takes the concept of genus as the basis of one's judgment. The tendency to judge according to the genus is at its most stubborn where we are concerned with differences of sex. Almost invariably man sees in woman, and woman in man, too much of the general character of the other sex and too little of what is individual. In practical life this does less harm to men than to women. The social position of women is for the most part such an unworthy one because in so many respects it is determined not as it should be by the particular characteristics of the individual woman, but by the general picture one has of woman's natural tasks and needs. A man's activity in life is governed by his individual capacities and inclinations, whereas a woman's is supposed to be determined solely by the mere fact that she is a woman. She is supposed to be a slave to what is generic, to womanhood in general. As long as men continue to debate whether a woman is suited to this or that profession "according to her natural disposition", the so-called woman's question cannot advance beyond its most elementary stage. What a woman, within her natural limitations, wants to become had better be left to the woman herself to decide. If it is true that women are suited only to that profession which is theirs at present, then they will hardly have it in them to attain any other. But they must be allowed to decide for themselves what is in accordance with their nature. To all who fear an upheaval of our social structure through accepting women as individuals and not as females, we must reply that a social structure in which the status of one half of humanity is unworthy of a human being is itself in great need of improvement.*

Anyone who judges people according to generic characters gets only as far as the frontier where people begin to be beings whose activity is based on free self-determination. Whatever lies short of this frontier may naturally become matter for academic study. The characteristics of race, people, nation and sex are the subject matter of special branches of study. Only men who wish to live as nothing more than examples of the genus could possibly conform to a general picture such as arises from academic study of this kind. But none of these branches of study are able to advance as far as the unique content of the single individual. Determining the individual according to the laws of his genus ceases where the sphere of freedom (in thinking and acting)

* Immediately upon the publication of this book (1894), critics objected to the above arguments that, even now, within the generic character of her sex, a woman is able to shape her life individually, just as she pleases, and far more freely than a man who is already de-individualized, first by the school, and later by war and profession. I am aware that this objection will be urged today (1918), even more strongly. None the less, I feel bound to let my sentences stand, in the hope that there are readers who appreciate how violently such an objection runs counter to the concept of freedom advocated in this book, and who will judge my sentences above by a standard other than the de-individualizing of man through school and profession.

begins. The conceptual content which man has to connect with the percept by an act of thinking in order to have the full reality (page 67 ff.) cannot be fixed once and for all and bequeathed ready-made to mankind. The individual must get his concepts through his own intuition. How the individual has to think cannot possibly be deduced from any kind of generic concept. It depends simply and solely on the individual. Just as little is it possible to determine from the general characteristics of man what concrete aims the individual may choose to set himself. If we would understand the single individual we must find our way into his own particular being and not stop short at those characteristics that are typical. In this sense every single human being is a separate problem. And every kind of study that deals with abstract thoughts and generic concepts is but a preparation for the knowledge we get when a human individuality tells us his way of viewing the world, and on the other hand for the knowledge we get from the content of his acts of will. Whenever we feel that we are dealing with that element in a man which is free from stereotyped thinking and instinctive willing, then, if we would understand him in his essence, we must cease to call to our aid any concepts at all of our own making. The act of knowing consists in combining the concept with the percept by means of thinking. With all other objects the observer must get his concepts through his intuition; but if we are to understand a free individuality we must take over into our own spirit those concepts by which he determines himself, in their pure form (without mixing our own conceptual content with them). Those who immediately mix their own concepts into every judgment about another person, can never arrive at the understanding of an individuality. Just as the free individuality emancipates himself from the characteristics of the genus, so must the act of knowing emancipate itself from the way in which we understand what is generic.

Only to the extent that a man has emancipated himself in this way from all that is generic, does he count as a free spirit within a human community. No man is all genus, none is all individuality. But every man gradually emancipates a greater or lesser sphere of his being, both from the generic characteristics of animal life and from domination by the decrees of human authorities.

As regards that part of his nature where a man is not able to achieve this freedom for himself, he constitutes a part of the whole organism of nature and spirit. In this respect he lives by copying others or by obeying their commands. But only that part of his conduct that springs from his intuitions can have ethical value in the true sense. And those moral instincts that he possesses through the inheritance of social instincts acquire ethical value through being taken up into his intuitions. It is from individual ethical intuitions and their acceptance by human communities that all moral activity of mankind originates. In other words, the moral life of mankind is the sum total of the products of the moral imagination of free human individuals. This is the conclusion reached by monism.

ULTIMATE QUESTIONS

The Consequences of Monism

THE uniform explanation of the world, that is, the monism we have described, derives the principles that it needs for the explanation of the world from human experience. In the same way, it looks for the sources of action within the world of observation, that is, in that part of human nature which is accessible to our self-knowledge, more particularly in moral imagination. Monism refuses to infer in an abstract way that the ultimate causes of the world that is presented to our perceiving and thinking are to be found in a region *outside* this world. For monism, the unity that thoughtful observation—which we *can* experience—brings to the manifold multiplicity of percepts is the same unity that man's need for knowledge demands, and through which it seeks entry into the physical and spiritual regions of the world. Whoever seeks another unity behind this one only proves that he does not recognize the identity of what is discovered by thinking and what is demanded by the urge for knowledge. The single human individual is not actually cut off from the universe. He is a part of it, and between this part and the totality of the cosmos there exists a real connection which is broken only for our perception. At first we take this part of the universe as something existing on its own, because we do not see the belts and ropes by which the fundamental forces of the cosmos keep the wheel of our life revolving.

Whoever remains at this standpoint sees a part of the whole as if it were actually an independently existing thing, a monad which receives information about the rest of the world in some way from without. Monism, as here described, shows that we can believe in this independence only so long as the things we perceive are not woven by our thinking into the network of the conceptual world. As soon as this happens, all separate existence turns out to be mere *illusion due to perceiving*. Man can find his full and complete existence in the totality of the universe only through the experience of intuitive thinking. Thinking destroys the illusion due to perceiving and integrates our individual existence into the life of the cosmos. The unity of the conceptual world, which contains all objective percepts, also embraces the content of our subjective personality. Thinking gives us reality in its true form as a self-contained unity, whereas the multiplicity of percepts is but a semblance due to the way we are organized (see page 67). To recognize true reality, as against the illusion due to perceiving, has at all times been the goal of human thinking. Scientific thought has made great efforts to recognize reality in percepts by discovering the systematic connections between them. Where, however, it was believed that the connections ascertained by human thinking had only subjective validity, the true basis of unity was sought in some entity lying beyond our world of experience (an inferred God, will, absolute spirit, etc.). On the strength of this belief, the attempt was made to obtain, in addition to the knowledge accessible to experience, a second kind of knowledge which transcends experience and shows how the world that *can* be experienced is connected with the entities that *cannot* (a metaphysics arrived at by inference, and not by experience). It was thought that the reason why we can grasp the connections of things in the world through disciplined thinking was that a primordial being had built the world upon logical laws, and, similarly, that the grounds for our actions lay in the will of such a being. What was not realized was that thinking embraces both the subjective and the objective in one grasp, and that through the union of percept with concept the full reality is conveyed. Only as long as we think of the law and order that permeates and determines the percept as having the abstract form of a concept, are we in fact dealing with something purely subjective. But the content of a concept, which is added to the percept by means of thinking, is not subjective. This content is not taken from the subject, but from reality. It is that part of the reality that cannot be reached by the act of perceiving. It is experience, but not experience gained through perceiving. If someone cannot see that the concept is something real, he is thinking of it only in the abstract form in which he holds it in his mind. But only through our organization is it present in such isolation, just as in the case of the percept. After all, the tree that one perceives has no existence by itself, in isolation. It exists only as a part of the immense machinery of nature, and *can* only exist in real connection with nature. An abstract concept taken by itself has as little reality as a percept taken by itself. The percept is the part of reality that is given objectively, the concept the part that is given subjectively (through intuition—see page 73 ff.). Our mental organization tears the reality apart into these two factors. One factor presents itself to perception, the other to intuition. Only the union of the two, that is, the percept fitting systematically into the universe, constitutes the full reality. If we take mere percepts by themselves, we have no reality but rather a disconnected chaos; if we take by itself the law and order connecting the percepts, then we have nothing but abstract concepts. Reality is not contained in the abstract concept; it is, however, contained in thoughtful observation, which does not one-sidedly consider either concept or percept alone, but rather the union of the two.

That we live in reality (that we are rooted in it with our real existence) will not be denied by even the most orthodox of subjective idealists. He will only deny that we reach the same reality with our knowing, with our ideas, as the one we actually live in. Monism, on the other hand, shows that thinking is neither subjective nor objective, but is a principle that embraces both sides of reality. When we observe with our thinking, we carry out a process which itself belongs to the order of real events. By means of thinking, within the experience itself, we overcome the one-sidedness of mere perceiving. We cannot argue out the essence of reality by means of abstract conceptual hypotheses (through pure conceptual reflection), but in so far as we find the ideas that belong to the percepts, we are *living* in the reality. Monism does not seek to add to experience something non-experienceable (transcendental), but finds the full reality in concept and percept. It does not spin a system of metaphysics out of mere abstract concepts, because it sees in the concept by itself only *one* side of the reality, namely, the side that remains hidden from perception, and only makes sense in connection with the percept. Monism does, however, give man the conviction that he lives in the world of reality and has no need to look beyond this world for a higher reality that can never be experienced. It refrains from seeking absolute reality anywhere else but in experience, because it is just in the content of experience that it recognizes reality. Monism is satisfied by this reality, because it knows that thinking has the power to guarantee it. What dualism seeks only beyond the observed world, monism finds in this world itself. Monism shows that with our act of knowing we grasp reality in its true form, and not as a subjective image that inserts itself between man and reality. For monism, the conceptual content of the world is the same for all human individuals (see page 68). According to monistic principles, one human individual regards another as akin to himself because the same world content expresses itself in him. In the unitary world of concepts there are not as many concepts of the lion as there are individuals who think of a lion, but only *one*. And the concept that A fits to his percept of the lion is the same that B fits to his, only apprehended by a different perceiving subject (see page 69). Thinking leads all perceiving subjects to the same ideal unity in all multiplicity. The unitary world of ideas expresses itself in them as in a multiplicity of individuals. As long as a man apprehends himself merely by means of self-perception, he sees himself as this particular man; as soon as he looks at the world of ideas that lights up within him, embracing all that is separate, he sees within himself the absolute reality living and shining forth. Dualism defines the divine primordial Being as that which pervades and lives in all men. Monism finds this divine life, common to all, in reality itself. The ideas of another human being are in substance mine also, and I regard them as different only as long as I perceive, but no longer when I think. Every man embraces in his thinking only a part of the total world of ideas, and to that extent individuals differ even in the actual content of their thinking. But all these contents are within a self-contained whole, which embraces the thought contents of all men. Hence every man, in his thinking, lays hold of the universal primordial Being which pervades all men. To live in reality, filled with the content of thought, is at the same time to live in God. A world beyond, that is merely inferred and cannot be experienced, arises from a misconception on the part of those who believe that *this* world cannot have the foundation of its existence within itself. They do not realize that through thinking they find just what they require for the explanation of the percept. This is the reason why no speculation has ever brought to light any content that was not borrowed from the reality given to us. The God that is assumed through abstract inference is nothing but a human being transplanted into the Beyond; Schopenhauer's Will is human will-power made absolute; Hartmann's Unconscious, a primordial Being made up of idea and will, is but a compound of two abstractions drawn from experience. Exactly the same is true of all other transcendental principles based on thought that has not been experienced.

The truth is that the human spirit never transcends the reality in which we live, nor has it any need to do so, seeing that this world contains everything the human spirit requires in order to explain it. If philosophers eventually declare themselves satisfied with the deduction of the world from principles they borrow from experience and transplant into an hypothetical Beyond, then it should be just as possible to be satisfied when the same content is allowed to remain in this world, where for our thinking as experienced it does belong. All attempts to transcend the world are purely illusory, and the principles transplanted from this world into the Beyond do not explain the world any better than those which remain within it. If thinking understands itself it will not ask for any such transcendence at all, since every content of thought must look within the world and not outside it for a perceptual content, together with which it forms something real. The objects of imagination, too, are no more than contents which become justified only when transformed into mental pictures that refer to a perceptual content. Through this perceptual content they become an integral part of reality. A concept that is supposed to be filled with a content lying beyond our given world is an abstraction to which no reality corresponds. We can think out only the *concepts* of reality; in order to find reality itself, we must also have perception. A primordial world being for which we *invent* a content is an impossible assumption for any thinking that understands itself. Monism does not deny ideal elements, in fact, it considers a perceptual content without an ideal counterpart as not fully real; but in the whole realm of thinking it finds nothing that could require us to step outside the realm of our thinking's experience by denying the objective spiritual reality of thinking itself. Monism regards a science that limits itself to a description of percepts without penetrating to their ideal complements as incomplete. But it regards as equally incomplete all abstract concepts that do not find their complements in percepts, and that fit nowhere into the conceptual network that embraces the whole observable world. Hence it knows no ideas that refer to objective factors lying beyond our experience and which are supposed to form the content of a purely hypothetical system of metaphysics. All that mankind has produced in the way of such ideas monism regards as abstractions borrowed from experience, the fact of borrowing having been overlooked by the originators.

Just as little, according to monistic principles, can the aims of our action be derived from an extra-human Beyond. In so far as we think them, they must stem from human intuition. Man does not take the purposes of an objective (transcendental) primordial Being and make them his own, but he pursues his own individual purposes given him by his moral imagination. The idea that realizes itself in an action is detached by man from the unitary world of ideas and made the basis of his will. Therefore it is not the commandments injected into this world from the Beyond that live in his action, but human intuitions belonging to this world itself. Monism knows no such world-dictator who sets our aims and directs our actions from outside. Man finds no such primal ground of existence whose counsels he might investigate in order to learn from it the aims to which he has to direct his actions. He is thrown back upon himself. It is he himself who must give content to his action. If he looks outside the world in which he lives for the grounds determining his will, he will look in vain. If he is to go beyond merely satisfying his natural instincts, for which Mother Nature has provided, then he must seek these grounds in his own moral imagination, unless he finds it more convenient to let himself be determined by the moral imaginations of others; in other words, either he must give up action altogether, or else he must act for reasons that he gives himself out of his world of ideas or that others select for him out of theirs. If he advances beyond merely following his life of sensuous instincts or carrying out the commands of others, then he will be determined by nothing but himself. He must act out of an impulse given by himself and determined by nothing else. It is true that this impulse is determined ideally in the unitary world of ideas; but in practice it is only by man that it can be taken from that world and translated into reality. The grounds for the actual translation of an idea into reality by man, monism can find only in man himself. If an idea is to become action, man must first *want* it, before it can happen. Such an act of will therefore has its grounds only in man himself. Man is then the ultimate determinant of his action. He is free.

Author's additions, 1918

1. In the second part of this book the attempt has been made to demonstrate that freedom is to be found in the reality of human action. For this purpose it was necessary to single out from the whole sphere of human conduct those actions in which, on the basis of unprejudiced self-observation, one can speak of freedom. These are actions that represent the realization of ideal intuitions. No other actions will be called free by an unprejudiced observer. Yet just by observing himself in an unprejudiced way, man will have to see that it is in his nature to progress along the road towards ethical intuitions and their realization. But *this* unprejudiced observation of the ethical nature of man cannot, by itself, arrive at a final conclusion about freedom. For were intuitive thinking to originate in anything other than itself, were its essence not self-sustaining, then the consciousness of freedom that flows from morality would prove to be a mere illusion. But the second part of this book finds its natural support in the first part. This presents intuitive thinking as man's inwardly experienced spiritual activity. To understand *this* nature of thinking by *experiencing* it amounts to a knowledge of the *freedom* of intuitive thinking. And once we know that this thinking is free, we can also see to what region of the will freedom may be ascribed. We shall regard man as a *free* agent if, on the basis of inner experience, we may attribute a self-sustaining essence to the life of intuitive thinking. Whoever cannot do this will never be able to discover a path to the acceptance of freedom that cannot be challenged in any way. This experience, to which we have attached such importance, discovers intuitive thinking

within consciousness, although the reality of this thinking is not confined to consciousness. And with this it discovers freedom as the distinguishing feature of all actions proceeding from the intuitions of consciousness.

2. The argument of this book is built upon intuitive thinking which may be experienced in a purely spiritual way and through which, in the act of knowing, every percept is placed in the world of reality. This book aims at presenting no more than can be surveyed through the experience of intuitive thinking. But we must also emphasize what kind of thought formation this experience of thinking demands. It demands that we shall not deny that intuitive thinking is a self-sustaining experience within the process of knowledge. It demands that we acknowledge that this thinking, in conjunction with the percept, is able to experience reality instead of having to seek it in an inferred world lying beyond experience, compared to which the activity of human thinking would be something purely subjective.

Thus thinking is characterized as that factor through which man works his way spiritually into reality. (And, actually, no one should confuse this world conception that is based on the direct experience of thinking with mere rationalism.) On the other hand, it should be evident from the whole spirit of this argument that for human knowledge the perceptual element only becomes a guarantee of reality when it is taken hold of in thinking. *Outside* thinking there is nothing to characterize reality for what it is. Hence we must not imagine that the kind of reality guaranteed by sense perception is the only one. Whatever comes to us by way of percept is something that, on our journey through life, we simply have to *await*. The only question is, would it be right to *expect*, from the point of view that this purely intuitively experienced thinking gives us, that man could *perceive* spiritual things as well as those perceived with the senses? It would be right to expect this. For although, *on the one hand*, intuitively experienced thinking is an active process taking place in the human spirit, *on the other hand* it is also a spiritual percept grasped without a physical sense organ. It is a percept in which the perceiver is himself active, and a self-activity which is at the same time perceived. In intuitively experienced thinking man is carried into a spiritual world also as perceiver. Within this spiritual world, whatever confronts him as percept in the same way that the spiritual world of his own thinking does will be recognized by him as a world of spiritual perception. *This* world of spiritual perception could be seen as having the same relationship to thinking that the world of sense perception has on the side of the senses. Once experienced, the world of spiritual perception cannot appear to man as something foreign to him, because in his intuitive thinking he already has an experience which is purely spiritual in character. Such a world of spiritual perception is discussed in a number of writings which I have published since this book first appeared. *The Philosophy of Freedom* forms the philosophical foundation for these later writings. For it tries to show that the experience of thinking, when rightly understood, *is* in fact an experience of spirit. Therefore it appears to the author that no one who can in all seriousness adopt the point of view of *The Philosophy of Freedom* will stop short before entering the world of spiritual perception. It is certainly not possible to deduce what is described in the author's later books by logical inference from the contents of this one. But a living comprehension of what is meant in this book by intuitive thinking will lead quite naturally to a living entry into the world of spiritual perception.

APPENDIX

Added to the new edition, 1918

OBJECTIONS which were made from the philosophical side immediately upon the publication of this book induce me to add the following brief discussion to this new edition.

I can well understand that there are readers who are interested in the rest of the book, but who will look upon what follows as a remote and unnecessary tissue of abstract concepts. They can leave this short statement unread. But in philosophy problems arise which have their origin more in certain prejudices on the thinkers' part than in the natural course of human thinking itself. Otherwise it seems to me that this book deals with a task that concerns *everyone* who is trying to get clear about the nature of man and his relationship to the world. What follows is rather a problem which certain philosophers insist should be discussed as part of the subject matter of such a book, because, by their whole way of thinking, they have created certain difficulties which do not otherwise occur. If one were to pass by such problems altogether, certain people would be quick to accuse one of dilettantism and the like. And the impression would arise that the author of the views set down in this book has not come to terms with those points of view he has not discussed in the book itself.

The problem to which I refer is this: there are thinkers who believe that a special difficulty arises when one tries to understand how another person's soul life can affect one's own. They say: my conscious world is enclosed within me; in the same way, any other conscious world is enclosed within itself. I cannot see into the world of consciousness of another person. How, then, do I know that he and I are both in the same world? The theory which believes it possible to infer from the conscious world an unconscious world which can never enter consciousness, tries to solve this difficulty in the following way. It says: the world I have in my consciousness is the representative in me of a real world to which I have no conscious access. In this real world lie the unknown causes of my conscious world. In it also lies my own real being, of which I have only a representative in my consciousness. In it also, however, lies the being of my fellow man. Now whatever is experienced in the consciousness of my fellow man corresponds to a reality in his being which is independent of his consciousness. This reality acts, in the realm which cannot become conscious, upon my own real being which is said to be unconscious; and in this way something is created in my consciousness representing what is present in a consciousness that is quite independent of my own conscious experience. It is clear that to the world accessible to my consciousness an inaccessible one is here being added hypothetically, since one believes that otherwise one is forced to the conclusion that the whole external world, which I think is there in front of me, is nothing but the world of my consciousness, and to the further—solipsistic— absurdity that other people, too, exist only within my consciousness.

This problem, which has been created by several recent tendencies in epistemology, can be clarified if one tries to survey the matter from the point of view of the spiritually orientated observation adopted in this book. What is it, in the first instance, that I have before me when I confront another person? The most immediate thing is the bodily appearance of the other person as given to me in sense perception; then, perhaps, the auditory perception of what he is saying, and so on. I do not merely stare at all this, but it sets my thinking activity in motion. Through the thinking with which I confront the other person, the percept of him becomes, as it were, transparent to the mind. I am bound to admit that when I grasp the percept with my thinking, it is not at all the same thing as appeared to the outer senses. In what is a direct appearance to the senses, something else is indirectly revealed. The mere sense appearance extinguishes itself at the same time as it confronts me. But what it reveals through this extinguishing compels me as a thinking being to extinguish my own thinking as long as I am under its influence, and to put *its* thinking in the place of mine. I then grasp *its* thinking in my thinking as an experience like my own. I have really perceived another person's thinking. The immediate percept, extinguishing itself as sense appearance, is grasped by my thinking, and this is a process lying wholly within my consciousness and consisting in this, that the other person's thinking takes the place of mine. Through the self-extinction of the sense appearance, the separation between the two spheres of consciousness is actually overcome. This expresses itself in my consciousness through the fact that while experiencing the content of another person's consciousness I experience my own consciousness as little as I experience it in dreamless sleep. Just as in dreamless sleep my waking consciousness is eliminated, so in my perceiving of the content of another person's consciousness the content of my own is eliminated. The illusion that it is not so only comes about because in perceiving the other person, firstly, the extinction of the content of one's own consciousness gives place not to unconsciousness, as it does in sleep, but to the content of the other person's consciousness, and secondly, the alternations between extinguishing and lighting up again of my own self-consciousness follow too rapidly to be generally noticed.

This whole problem is to be solved, not through artificial conceptual structures with inferences from the conscious to things that can never become conscious, but rather through genuine experience of what results from combining thinking with the percept. This applies to a great many problems which appear in philosophical literature. Thinkers should seek the path to open-minded, spiritually orientated observation; instead of which they insert an artificial conceptual structure between themselves and the reality.

In a treatise by Eduard von Hartmann entitled *The Ultimate Problems of Epistemology and Metaphysics,** my *Philosophy of Freedom* has been classed with the philosophical tendency which would base itself upon an "epistemological monism". Eduard von Hartmann rejects such a position as untenable. This is explained as follows. According to the way of thinking expressed in his treatise, there are only three possible positions in the theory of knowledge.

Firstly, one remains at the naïve point of view, which regards perceived phenomena as real things existing outside human consciousness. This implies a lack of critical knowledge. One fails to realize that with the content of one's consciousness one remains, after all, only within one's own consciousness. One fails to perceive that one is dealing, not with a "table-in-itself", but only with an object in one's own consciousness. Whoever remains at this point of view, or for whatever reason returns to it, is a naïve realist. But this whole position is untenable for it fails to recognize that consciousness has no other objects than its own contents.

* *"Die letzten Fragen der Erkenntnistheorie und Metaphysik"*, *Zeitschrift für Philosophie und philosophische Kritik*, Vol. 108, p. 55.

Secondly, one appreciates this situation and admits it fully to oneself. One would then be a transcendental idealist. But then one would have to deny that anything of a "thing-in-itself" could ever appear in human consciousness. In this way, however, provided one is consistent enough, one will not avoid absolute illusionism. For the world which confronts one now transforms itself into a mere sum of objects of consciousness, and, moreover, only of objects of one's own consciousness. One is then compelled—absurdly enough—to regard other people too as being present solely in the content of one's own consciousness.

The only possible standpoint is the third, transcendental realism. This assumes that there are "things-in-themselves", but that the consciousness can have no kind of dealings with them in immediate experience. Beyond the sphere of human consciousness, and in a way that does not enter it, they cause the objects of our consciousness to arise in it. One can arrive at these "things-in-themselves" only by inference from the content of consciousness, which is all that is actually experienced but is nevertheless merely pictured in the mind.

Eduard von Hartmann maintains in the article mentioned above that "epistemological monism"—for such he takes my point of view to be—must in reality accept one of these three positions; and it fails to do so only because it does not draw the logical conclusions from its postulates. The article goes on to say:

> If one wants to find out which theoretical position a supposed epistemological monist occupies, one need only put certain questions to him and compel him to answer them. For such a person will never willingly commit himself to an expression of opinion on these points, and will, moreover, seek by all means to evade answering direct questions, because

every answer would show that epistemological monism cannot claim to be different from one or other of the three positions. These questions are as follows:

(1) Are things *continuous* or *intermittent* in their existence? If the answer is "continuous", then one is dealing with some form of naïve realism. If the answer is "intermittent", then one has transcendental idealism. But if the answer is that they are, on the one hand, continuous (as contents of the absolute consciousness, or as unconscious mental pictures, or as possibilities of perception), but on the other hand, intermittent (as contents of limited consciousness), then transcendental realism is established.

(2) When three people are sitting at a table, *how many distinct tables* are there? Whoever answers "one" is a naïve realist; whoever answers "three" is a transcendental idealist; but whoever answers "four" is a transcendental realist. Here, of course, it is assumed that it is legitimate to embrace such different things as the one table as a thing-in-itself and the three tables as perceptual objects in the three consciousnesses under the common designation of "a table". If this seems too great a liberty to anyone, he will have to answer "one and three" instead of "four".

(3) When two people are alone together in a room, *how many distinct persons* are there? Whoever answers "two" is a naïve realist. Whoever answers "four" (namely, one self and one other person in each of the two consciousnesses) is a transcendental idealist. Whoever answers "six" (namely, two persons as "things-in-themselves" and four persons as mentally pictured objects in the two consciousnesses) is a transcendental realist.

If anyone wants to show that epistemological monism is different from any of these three positions, he would have to give a different answer to each of these three questions; but I would not know what this could be.

The answers of the *Philosophy of Freedom* would have to be:

(1) Whoever grasps only the perceptual contents of things and takes these for reality, is a naïve realist, and he does not realize that, strictly, he ought to regard *these perceptual contents* as existing only as long as he is looking at the things, so that he ought to think of the things before him as intermittent. As soon, however, as it becomes clear to him that reality is present only in the percepts that are permeated by thought, he will see that the perceptual contents which appear as *intermittent* reveal themselves as continuous as soon as they are permeated with the results of thinking. Hence we must count as continuous the perceptual content that has been grasped through the experience of thinking, of which only that part that is merely perceived could be regarded as intermittent, if—which is not the case—it were real.

(2) When three people are sitting at a table, how many distinct tables are there? There is only *one* table present; but as long as the three people went no further than their perceptual images, they would have to say, "*These* perceptual images are not a reality at all." As soon as they pass on to the table as grasped by their thinking, the *one* reality of the table reveals itself to them; then, with their three contents of consciousness, they are united in this reality.

(3) When two people are alone together in a room, how many distinct persons are there? There are most certainly not six—not even in the sense of the transcendental realists—but only two. All one can say is that, at the first moment, each person has nothing but the unreal perceptual image of himself and of the other person. There are four of these *images*, and through their presence in the thinking activity of the two people, reality is grasped. In this activity of thinking each person transcends his own sphere of consciousness; in it the consciousness of the other person as

well as of himself comes to life. In these moments of coming
to life the two people are as little enclosed within their own
consciousnesses as they are in sleep. But at other moments
the awareness of the absorption in the other person appears
again, so that the consciousness of each person, in the
experience of thinking, apprehends both himself and the
other. I know that a transcendental realist describes this as a
relapse into naïve realism. But then, I have already pointed
out in this book that naïve realism retains its justification for
the thinking that is experienced.

The transcendental realist will have nothing whatever to
do with the true state of affairs regarding the process of
knowledge; he cuts himself off from the facts by a tissue of
thoughts and entangles himself in it. Moreover, the monism
which appears in *The Philosophy of Freedom* ought not to be
labelled "epistemological", but, if an epithet is wanted,
then a "monism of thought". All this has been misunderstood by Eduard von Hartmann. He has ignored all that is
specific in the argumentation of *The Philosophy of Freedom*,
and has stated that I have attempted to combine Hegel's
universalistic panlogism with Hume's individualistic
phenomenalism,* whereas in fact *The Philosophy of Freedom*
has nothing whatever to do with the two positions it is
allegedly trying to combine. (This, too, is the reason why I
could not feel inclined, for example, to go into the
"epistemological monism" of Johannes Rehmke. The point
of view of *The Philosophy of Freedom* is simply quite different
from what Eduard von Hartmann and others call epistemological monism.)

* *Zeitschrift für Philosophie*, Vol. 108, p. 71, note.

Translator's Note:

In the revised edition of 1918, a revised version of the original preface of 1894 was placed at the end of the book as a second appendix. In this edition, following normal English practice, it is placed immediately after the new preface at the beginning of the book (see page xxvii).

INDEX

(Names of authors cited in the text)